Great Taste ~ Low Fat

HEARTY SOUPS & STEWS

TIME
LIFE
BOOKS

ALEXANDRIA, VIRGINIA

TABLE OF CONTENTS

Spicy Beer-Braised Beef Stew

page 69

Hearty Turkey Chowder

page 150

INTRODUCTION

The very image of home cooking is embodied in the making of a soup or stew "from scratch." It's the image of someone standing at the stove—tasting, adding a pinch of this or a dash of that, stirring, straining, and skimming—that sounds like a lot of work. But you can make terrific soups in less than an hour, and with the failsafe recipes in this book, there's never any guesswork involved.

NEW TWISTS ON OLD FAVORITES

Our chef, Sandy Gluck, cherishes memories of old-fashioned soups lovingly prepared by her mother, grandmothers, and aunts. "Sure, there was canned soup in our kitchen, but it was just for emergencies," says Sandy. Barley soup, beef stew, and vegetable soup with macaroni are three of her favorites, although these days she updates them a bit when cooking for her own family. Sandy often experiments with flavors: "With beef stew, for instance, you can take the dish in a different direction by using Mexican or Indian or Italian seasonings." Sandy also knows how to cut the fat in classic recipes. "Soups and stews often call for tough but fatty cuts of meat that will be tenderized by long simmering. Instead, I use lean cuts and quickly sauté them, which keeps them tender and flavorful. Where my grandmother used

brisket, for instance, I use top round. And I like to thicken soups by puréeing a portion of the vegetables and then stirring them back in. This intensifies the flavor, where the traditional addition of cream would dilute it."

Classic recipes make a fine starting point, but Sandy's versions of the old favorites often present pleasant surprises. The seasonings range from the expected—pungent rosemary and sage; perfumy fresh basil, mint, and dill; and dried oregano and thyme—to the more exotic curry powder, ginger, allspice, coriander, and cinnamon, to name a few. In addition to familiar soup vegetables like potatoes, onions, carrots, celery, turnips, and parsnips (all nutritionally praiseworthy), you'll find some new ideas for soup and stew ingredients in this book: butternut squash, rutabaga, watercress, snow peas, spinach, pearl onions, and even apples, bananas, and apricots. We can't think of a more delicious way to consume your recommended five daily servings of fruits and vegetables.

SOMETHING FOR EVERYONE

Our Chicken & Turkey chapter includes recipes from all over the world: From Morocco to Mexico, Italy to the Caribbean, poultry is used in ingenious ways to make a delightful variety of soups and stews. Our Beef, Pork & Lamb recipes are substantial but not stodgy: Classic beef and lamb stews appear in a number of styles, and you'll also find new takes on those all-American favorites, gumbo and chili. The recipes found in the chapter titled Vegetables are not just for vegetarians. Soups replete with beans, lentils, barley, bulghur, winter squash, or filled pasta can be every bit as hearty as those made with meat. Our Fish & Shellfish recipes run the gamut from a light, distinctively spicy Asian-Style Shrimp Soup and an elegant Crab Bisque to homestyle seafood chowders and stews, including San Francisco's famous Cioppino. In the final chapter, Big Batches, you'll find recipes that make eight servings rather than four. Use them for entertaining (a soup supper makes a cozy, casual party) or freeze half the batch to serve another day.

A number of recipes throughout the book are designed for the slow cooker, an ingenious appliance that lets you simmer a soup or stew all day long whether you're at home or away.

Our "Secrets of Low-Fat Cooking" section clues you in to the ingredients that make soups, stews, and chowders tasty and satisfying; we also supply suggestions on how to freeze and thaw soup, and how to thicken low-fat soups by using starchy ingredients or a variety of techniques.

CONTRIBUTING EDITORS

Sandra Rose Gluck, a New York City chef, has years of experience creating delicious low-fat recipes that are quick to prepare. Her secret for satisfying results is to always aim for great taste and variety. By combining readily available, fresh ingredients with simple cooking techniques, Sandra has created the perfect recipes for today's busy lifestyles.

Grace Young has been the director of a major test kitchen specializing in low-fat and health-related cookbooks for over 12 years. Grace oversees the development, taste testing, and nutritional analysis of every recipe in Great Taste–Low Fat. Her goal is simple: take the work and worry out of low-fat cooking so that you can enjoy delicious, healthy meals every day.

Kate Slate has been a food editor for almost 20 years, and has published thousands of recipes in cookbooks and magazines. As the Editorial Director of Great Taste–Low Fat, Kate combined simple, easy to follow directions with practical low-fat cooking tips. The result is guaranteed to make your low-fat cooking as rewarding and fun as it is foolproof.

NUTRITION

Every recipe in *Great Taste–Low Fat* provides per-serving values for the nutrients listed in the chart at right. The daily intakes listed in the chart are based on those recommended by the USDA and presume a nonsedentary lifestyle. The nutritional emphasis in this book is not only on controlling calories, but on reducing total fat grams. Research has shown that dietary fat metabolizes more easily into body fat than do carbohydrates and protein. In order to control the amount of fat in a given recipe and in your diet in general, no more than 30 percent of the calories should come from fat.

Nutrient	Women	Men
Fat	<65 g	<80 g
Calories	2000	2500
Saturated fat	<20 g	<25 g
Carbohydrate	300 g	375 g
Protein	50 g	65 g
Cholesterol	<300 mg	<300 mg
Sodium	<2400 mg	<2400 mg

These recommended daily intakes are averages used by the Food and Drug Administration and are consistent with the labeling on all food products. Although the values for cholesterol and sodium are the same for all adults, the other intake values vary depending on gender, ideal weight, and activity level. Check with a physician or nutritionist for your own daily intake values.

SECRETS OF LOW-FAT COOKING

LOW-FAT SOUPS AND STEWS

There's no meal quite as warming and comforting on a winter night as one that centers on a steaming pot of soup or stew. In other seasons, too, a hearty soup can take the edge off a chilly evening and amply satisfy the appetites of a hungry family.

But traditional soups are often high in fat, because they're made with generous amounts of butter, heavy cream, bacon, sausage, and the like. By employing smart substitutions (such as evaporated skimmed milk for cream) and creative techniques (puréeing vegetables to thicken the broth, for example), we've preserved the old-fashioned flavors while holding the fat content of these main-dish soups at healthy levels.

HEARTY INGREDIENTS

The great thing about soups and stews is that all the goodness of the ingredients—the savory richness of browned meat, the thickening starch of grains, the fresh flavors and abundant nutrients in vegetables—ends up in the finished dish. That's also why it's important to start with lean components: Any fat that goes in, stays in.

• **Meats.** Lean meats such as skinless chicken, beef round, lamb shoulder, and pork tenderloin can be just as flavorful as fattier cuts; dredging the meat with flour and browning it (a technique used in many of our recipes) really brings out the flavor in the meat.

• **Grains and pasta.** A handful of rice, quick-cooking barley, or bulghur can turn a brothy soup into something substantial, both by adding carbohydrates and by releasing starch into the soup. Small pasta shapes such as ditalini or orzo, noodles, or strand-shaped pastas such as spaghetti or linguine also add dimension to simple soups.

• **Vegetables.** These play a number of roles in soup making. Some, such as onion, garlic, leek, scallion, and tomato, seem to melt away as the soup cooks, but their intense flavors linger on. Mushroom and eggplant have a dense, meaty texture that "beefs up" meatless soups. Root vegetables like potato and turnip, as well as starchy winter squash, form the sturdy underpinnings of many stews; their starches also thicken the liquid they're cooked in (see page 8 for information on thickening soups). Fresh vegetables like peas and corn offer a delicately crisp contrast to more tender ingredients. Be careful not to overcook them or you'll lose that wonderful texture.

• **Dried beans, peas, and lentils.** Whether you simmer a soup or stew based on dried beans in a slow cooker or empty a handy can of beans into a quick chili, you're making a super-satisfying meal and using some of the healthiest ingredients possible. Because they're high in protein, beans, chickpeas, lentils, and the like can take the place of meat (with a fraction of the fat), and they also offer lots of vitamins, minerals, and dietary fiber. When using canned beans, always rinse them to wash away excess sodium.

FREEZING AND REHEATING

Many soups and stews are good candidates for advance preparation: If refrigerated (overnight or for up to a week), flavors blend and mellow. Most of the soups and stews in this book can also be frozen for up to a month. The exceptions are those that include fish and shellfish; potatoes also tend to turn mushy when frozen. Be careful not to overcook a soup or stew you're planning to freeze, since it will cook further when reheated.

If the structure of the recipe permits, add delicate ingredients, such as fresh greens or herbs, during the reheating rather than before freezing the soup or stew. The same goes for last-minute additions of milk or yogurt. When freezing soup, quick-chill it as soon as it's done by placing the pot in a basin of cold water. Thaw soup in the refrigerator before reheating it, and add a little liquid if, when reheated, the soup is too thick.

THICKENERS

Flours and meals are traditional low-fat thickeners for soups and stews. Because these powdery ingredients may form lumps when added to hot liquid, they are usually first mixed with cool liquid and then stirred into the pot.

• **Cornmeal.** Often used in Mexican cuisine, cornmeal becomes quite thick when cooked. Keep stirring as you add the cornmeal mixture to the soup.

• **Flour.** When flour is used, the soup or stew should be simmered for a few minutes longer so that the finished dish does not taste of raw flour.

• **Tapioca.** Constant stirring is not required when you use tapioca as a thickener. It comes in several forms; we use the quick-cooking ("instant") type.

• **Cornstarch.** This superfine corn flour leaves the soup glossy and transparent. Overcooking will thin a cornstarch-thickened mixture.

Starchy vegetables such as potatoes, legumes (such as dried beans, peas, or lentils), and grains (like rice, bulghur, or barley) thicken soups and stews with their natural starches, which are released as they cook. Okra makes a unique contribution to soups (most famously, gumbos): It releases a sticky substance that thickens the liquid it's cooked in.

Purées as Thickeners

To create thick, satisfying soups without resorting to such traditional high-fat additions as egg yolks, butter, or cream, just cook the vegetables and/or grains in the soup until they are tender and then purée them.

To lightly thicken a soup, simply mash some of the ingredients against the side of the pot with a fork, leaving the rest chunky. Or purée some of the vegetables (along with enough liquid for the machine to run smoothly) in a food processor or blender and then stir the purée back into the soup. For a totally "creamed" result, transfer the soup—in batches, if necessary—to a food processor or blender and purée it; you may need to reheat the soup slightly after processing it.

Alternatively, a hand blender (see right) can be used directly in the soup pot to either partially or fully purée a soup.

Using a Hand Blender

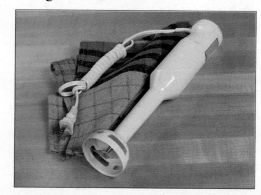

The hand blender, also called an immersion blender, is a useful new arrival in the kitchen. You can use it as you would an electric mixer, but it has a powerful sharp blade rather than beaters. With a hand blender, you can purée soups or mash potatoes right in the pot; you can also use it in a beaker to make healthy shakes or to chop nuts.

CHICKEN & TURKEY

1

CHICKEN VEGETABLE CHOWDER

SERVES: 4
WORKING TIME: 20 MINUTES
TOTAL TIME: 30 MINUTES

Two kinds of corn contribute to the pleasingly varied texture of this satisfying chowder. The frozen corn kernels retain a slightly crisp bite, while the creamed corn enhances the velvety quality of the broth. For lovely color, sweet potatoes replace the usual white potatoes in the chowder.

13¾-ounce can reduced-sodium chicken broth, defatted

¾ pound sweet potatoes, peeled and cut into ¾-inch cubes

1 teaspoon dried thyme

½ teaspoon dried rosemary

¼ teaspoon salt

¾ pound skinless, boneless chicken breasts, cut into ¾-inch chunks

2 cups coarsely chopped broccoli florets

6 tablespoons slivered Canadian bacon (2 ounces)

14¾-ounce can creamed corn

1 cup frozen corn kernels

⅓ cup reduced-fat sour cream

1. In a Dutch oven or flameproof casserole, combine the broth, 1 cup of water, the sweet potatoes, thyme, rosemary, and salt. Bring to a boil over high heat, reduce the heat to a simmer, and cook until the sweet potatoes are firm-tender, about 6 minutes. Add the chicken and broccoli and simmer until the chicken is cooked through, about 3 minutes.

2. Stir in the Canadian bacon, creamed corn, and frozen corn. Return to a simmer and cook until the sweet potatoes are tender and the corn is heated through, about 2 minutes. Remove from the heat, stir in the sour cream, and serve.

Helpful hints: The chowder should be quite thick, but if you'd like it thinner, stir in up to 1 cup of boiling water at the end of step 1. Use the leftover broccoli stalks to make a quick soup for another meal: Chop the stems and steam them until very tender, then purée in a food processor or blender. Thin the purée with low-fat milk and season with salt, pepper, and nutmeg.

FAT: 6G/15%
CALORIES: 353
SATURATED FAT: 2.1G
CARBOHYDRATE: 48G
PROTEIN: 32G
CHOLESTEROL: 63MG
SODIUM: 993MG

This
may look like a simple
tomato soup, but sniff
its rich aroma, then
sample a spoonful, and
you'll be happily
surprised. The soup is
a blend of tomatoes,
red peppers, and
onions, all roasted to
bring out their richest,
deepest flavor. Gently
herbed turkey
meatballs make the
soup a hearty meal.
Serve with a loaf of
peasant bread.

Roasted Vegetable Soup with Turkey Meatballs

Serves: 4
Working time: 30 minutes
Total time: 45 minutes

1 red onion, thickly sliced

1½ pounds plum tomatoes, halved lengthwise

2 red bell peppers, halved lengthwise and seeded

6 ounces lean ground turkey

¼ cup plain dried bread crumbs

¼ cup low-fat (1%) milk

⅛ teaspoon freshly ground black pepper

6 tablespoons chopped fresh basil

13¾-ounce can reduced-sodium chicken broth, defatted

1 tablespoon balsamic vinegar

1 clove garlic, minced

2 teaspoons paprika

½ teaspoon salt

1. Preheat the broiler. Place the onion slices, tomatoes, and bell peppers, cut-sides down, on a broiler pan and broil 4 inches from the heat for 12 minutes, or until the pepper and tomato skins are blackened. When cool enough to handle, peel the tomatoes and bell peppers (see tip).

2. Meanwhile, in a medium bowl, combine the ground turkey, bread crumbs, milk, black pepper, and 2 tablespoons of the basil, stirring to thoroughly blend. Shape the turkey mixture into ¾-inch balls, using about 1 rounded teaspoon per ball.

3. Transfer the broiled vegetables to a food processor or blender and purée until smooth, about 1 minute. Pour the vegetable purée into a large saucepan along with the broth, vinegar, garlic, paprika, and salt. Bring to a simmer and cook for 3 minutes to blend the flavors. Drop the meatballs into the simmering soup and cook until they are cooked through, about 5 minutes. Stir in the remaining ¼ cup basil, divide among 4 bowls, and serve.

Helpful hint: The turkey mixture should be mixed with a light hand (toss the ingredients together with two forks) and not tightly compacted (roll it lightly between your palms); otherwise, the meatballs will be tough.

Fat: 5g/26%
Calories: 173
Saturated Fat: 1.1g
Carbohydrate: 22g
Protein: 13g
Cholesterol: 32mg
Sodium: 669mg

TIP

Remove the skin from the roasted tomatoes and bell peppers by grasping it with your fingers and pulling it away from the flesh; the blackened skin will be quite loose. If necessary, scrape off any stubborn patches with a knife.

PEPPERY CHICKEN STEW

SERVES: 4
WORKING TIME: 30 MINUTES
TOTAL TIME: 30 MINUTES

1 cup long-grain rice

¾ teaspoon salt

3 tablespoons flour

1 teaspoon curry powder

1 teaspoon ground ginger

1 teaspoon ground cumin

⅛ teaspoon cayenne pepper

4 skinless, boneless chicken breast halves (about 1 pound total), cut crosswise into thirds

2 teaspoons olive oil

1 red bell pepper, cut into thin strips

1 green bell pepper, cut into thin strips

1 red onion, halved and thinly sliced

2 cloves garlic, minced

1 cup reduced-sodium chicken broth, defatted

2 tablespoons peanut butter

1. In a medium saucepan, bring 2¼ cups of water to a boil. Add the rice and ¼ teaspoon of the salt, reduce to a simmer, cover, and cook until the rice is tender, about 17 minutes.

2. Meanwhile, on a sheet of waxed paper, combine the flour, curry powder, ginger, cumin, cayenne, and the remaining ½ teaspoon salt. Dredge the chicken in the flour mixture, shaking off and reserving the excess. In a large nonstick saucepan, heat 1½ teaspoons of the oil until hot but not smoking over medium heat. Add the chicken and cook, stirring, until lightly browned all over, about 6 minutes. With a slotted spoon, transfer the chicken to a plate.

3. Add the remaining ½ teaspoon oil to the pan along with the bell peppers, onion, and garlic. Cook until the vegetables are softened, about 5 minutes. Sprinkle the reserved flour mixture over the vegetables, stirring until the flour is no longer visible. Add the broth and peanut butter, stirring to blend. Return the chicken to the pan, cover, and simmer until the chicken is cooked through, about 5 minutes. Divide the rice among 4 bowls, spoon the chicken mixture over, and serve.

Helpful hint: If you like your stew extra spicy, you can add an additional ⅛ teaspoon cayenne pepper to the dredging mixture in step 2.

FAT: 8G/17%
CALORIES: 422
SATURATED FAT: 1.4G
CARBOHYDRATE: 51G
PROTEIN: 35G
CHOLESTEROL: 66MG
SODIUM: 694MG

This chicken stew, made with peanut butter and warmly fragrant spices, traces its heritage back to West Africa, where peanuts are often used in savory dishes. Although peanut butter is high in fat, its flavor is so powerful that just a couple of spoonfuls suffice. The super-chunky stew is served over rice for a healthy carbohydrate balance.

CREAMY CHICKEN STEW WITH MUSHROOMS

A

slow cooker is a lifesaver on busy days, and the long cooking time yields a stew with beautifully melded flavors.

1 cup evaporated low-fat (1%) milk

¼ cup flour

4 whole chicken legs (about 1½ pounds total), split into drumsticks and thighs, skinned

¾ pound small mushrooms

3 cups frozen pearl onions

2 large carrots, halved lengthwise and cut into 1-inch chunks

2 cups frozen peas

1 cup reduced-sodium chicken broth, defatted

½ teaspoon salt

½ teaspoon dried marjoram

¼ teaspoon dried rosemary

¼ teaspoon freshly ground black pepper

¼ cup chopped fresh parsley

1. In a small bowl, combine the evaporated milk and flour, stirring until smooth.

2. In a 4-quart electric slow cooker, combine the chicken, mushrooms, pearl onions, carrots, peas, broth, milk mixture, salt, marjoram, rosemary, and pepper. Cover, and with the setting on low, cook until the chicken is cooked through and tender, 6 to 8 hours.

3. Stir the parsley into the stew before serving.

Helpful hint: Baby carrots, sold washed, peeled, and ready to use in bags, can be substituted for the cut-up carrots. Use 1 cup of the baby carrots.

FAT: 5G/13%
CALORIES: 352
SATURATED FAT: 1.1G
CARBOHYDRATE: 44G
PROTEIN: 33G
CHOLESTEROL: 84MG
SODIUM: 705MG

TURKEY CACCIATORE STEW

SERVES: 4
WORKING TIME: 40 MINUTES
TOTAL TIME: 40 MINUTES

2 teaspoons olive oil

2 onions, halved and thinly sliced

¾ pound mushrooms, thinly sliced

2 cloves garlic, minced

14½-ounce can no-salt-added stewed tomatoes

8-ounce can no-salt-added tomato sauce

¼ cup dry red wine

¼ cup chopped fresh basil or parsley, or 1 teaspoon dried basil

¾ teaspoon salt

½ teaspoon hot pepper sauce

¾ pound turkey cutlets, cut into 2 x 1-inch strips

6 ounces fettuccine

1. Start heating a large pot of water to boiling for the pasta. Meanwhile, in a large nonstick saucepan, heat the oil until hot but not smoking over medium heat. Add the onions and cook until softened, about 5 minutes. Add the mushrooms and garlic, increase the heat to high, and cook, stirring, until the liquid evaporates and the mushrooms are golden, about 5 minutes.

2. Add the stewed tomatoes, tomato sauce, wine, basil, salt, and hot pepper sauce to the pan. Bring to a boil, reduce the heat to a simmer, and cook until the flavors are blended, about 5 minutes. Add the turkey strips, stirring to coat with the sauce. Cover and cook until the turkey is cooked through, about 5 minutes.

3. Meanwhile, cook the fettuccine in the boiling water until just tender. Drain well. Divide the pasta among 4 bowls, spoon the turkey mixture over, and serve.

Helpful hint: Like many stews, this one is even better the second day. Reheat it gently, adding a little water if the stew has thickened, while you cook the pasta.

FAT: 6G/14%
CALORIES: 391
SATURATED FAT: 0.9G
CARBOHYDRATE: 53G
PROTEIN: 32G
CHOLESTEROL: 93MG
SODIUM: 516MG

Here's a new look for an all-time favorite: This easy cacciatore is made with strips of turkey instead of chicken parts.

MEXICAN TOMATO AND TORTILLA SOUP

SERVES: 4
WORKING TIME: 15 MINUTES
TOTAL TIME: 25 MINUTES

Mexican cooks sometimes use crisped tortilla strips in place of soup noodles, adding both heartiness and a textural contrast. Each bowl of this well-spiced soup brims with Mexican flavors—jalapeño, lime juice, cumin, cayenne, sweet corn, and tangy jack cheese.

2 teaspoons olive oil

Four 6-inch corn tortillas, cut into ½-inch-wide strips

4 scallions, thinly sliced

3 cloves garlic, minced

1 jalapeño pepper, seeded and minced

2 large tomatoes, coarsely chopped

8-ounce can no-salt-added tomato sauce

2 cups reduced-sodium chicken broth, defatted

1 teaspoon ground cumin

¼ teaspoon salt

⅛ teaspoon cayenne pepper

1 pound skinless, boneless chicken breasts, cut crosswise into ¼-inch-wide strips

1 cup frozen corn kernels

1 tablespoon fresh lime juice

3 tablespoons shredded Monterey jack cheese

1. In a nonstick Dutch oven or flameproof casserole, heat the oil until hot but not smoking over medium heat. Add the tortilla strips and cook until lightly crisped, about 1 minute. With a slotted spoon, transfer the strips to paper towels to drain.

2. Add the scallions, garlic, and jalapeño to the pan and cook until the scallions are softened, about 1 minute. Stir in the tomatoes, tomato sauce, broth, cumin, salt, and cayenne and bring to a boil. Reduce to a simmer, cover, and cook until the flavors are blended, about 5 minutes.

3. Add the chicken and corn, cover, and cook until the chicken is just cooked through, about 3 minutes. Stir in the tortilla strips and lime juice. Ladle into 4 soup bowls, sprinkle with the cheese, and serve.

Helpful hint: There's no need to cut each tortilla individually: You'll save time if you stack them and cut them all at once with a heavy knife.

FAT: 7G/20%
CALORIES: 313
SATURATED FAT: 1.8G
CARBOHYDRATE: 31G
PROTEIN: 34G
CHOLESTEROL: 72MG
SODIUM: 624MG

Dumplings
—what a treat! Fluffy and light, laced with bits of scallion, these baking-powder dumplings are sitting pretty atop an old-fashioned chicken-and-vegetable stew. While not quite as sensitive as a soufflé, dumplings are best if served as soon as they're made. Have a salad or any other accompaniments ready before you drop the dumpling dough into the stew.

CHICKEN STEW WITH ONION DUMPLINGS

SERVES: 4
WORKING TIME: 20 MINUTES
TOTAL TIME: 35 MINUTES

1¼ cups flour

½ cup evaporated skimmed milk

½ teaspoon hot pepper sauce

¼ teaspoon salt

4 teaspoons olive oil

2 ribs celery, chopped

1 onion, chopped

1 cup peeled baby carrots, halved lengthwise

¾ pound skinless, boneless chicken thighs, cut into ¾-inch cubes

1½ teaspoons Italian seasoning, or 1 teaspoon dried thyme and ½ teaspoon dried basil

13¾-ounce can reduced-sodium chicken broth, defatted

1 cup frozen peas

¾ cup skim milk

4 scallions, chopped

½ cup plain dried bread crumbs

2 teaspoons baking powder

1 teaspoon dry mustard

1. In a jar with a tight-fitting lid, combine ¼ cup of the flour, the evaporated milk, hot pepper sauce, and salt and shake to blend.

2. In a large, deep nonstick skillet, heat 1 teaspoon of the oil until hot but not smoking over medium heat. Add the celery, onion, and carrots and cook, stirring occasionally, until the vegetables are softened, about 8 minutes. Add the chicken and Italian seasoning and cook until the chicken is no longer pink, about 4 minutes. Add the broth and ⅓ cup of water and bring to a simmer. Shake the reserved evaporated milk mixture to recombine and stir the mixture into the pan. Bring to a simmer and cook until slightly thickened and creamy, about 3 minutes. Stir in the peas.

3. Meanwhile, in a medium bowl, combine the remaining 1 tablespoon oil, the skim milk, and scallions. With a wooden spoon, stir in the remaining 1 cup flour, the bread crumbs, baking powder, and mustard. With a large spoon, drop the dough into 12 dumplings on top of the simmering stew (see tip). Cover and cook until the chicken and dumplings are cooked through, about 8 minutes. Divide the chicken mixture and dumplings among 4 bowls and serve.

Helpful hint: If your skillet does not have a lid, lightly spray a sheet of foil large enough to fit over the skillet with nonstick cooking spray and carefully cover the skillet with it.

FAT: 10G/20%
CALORIES: 454
SATURATED FAT: 1.8G
CARBOHYDRATE: 60G
PROTEIN: 31G
CHOLESTEROL: 73MG
SODIUM: 991MG

TIP

Drop the dumpling dough onto the simmering chicken mixture, spacing the dumplings about 1 inch apart. For the lightest dumplings, do not uncover the skillet until the full cooking time has elapsed. Dumplings are done when a toothpick inserted into the center comes out clean and they feel firm to the touch.

GREEK-STYLE CHICKEN WITH RED SAUCE

SERVES: 4
WORKING TIME: 40 MINUTES
TOTAL TIME: 50 MINUTES

2 tablespoons flour

½ teaspoon salt

¼ teaspoon freshly ground black pepper

4 bone-in chicken breast halves (about 1½ pounds total), skinned and halved crosswise

1 tablespoon olive oil

8 ounces orzo

1 large onion, cut into 1-inch chunks

1 Granny Smith apple, halved, cored, and cut into 1-inch chunks

1 tomato, coarsely chopped

½ cup reduced-sodium chicken broth, defatted

¼ cup chopped fresh mint

1 tablespoon red wine vinegar

½ teaspoon cinnamon

1. On a sheet of waxed paper, combine the flour, ¼ teaspoon of the salt, and the pepper. Dredge the chicken in the flour mixture, shaking off the excess. In a nonstick Dutch oven or flameproof casserole, heat the oil until hot but not smoking over medium heat. Add the chicken and cook until golden brown, about 4 minutes per side. With a slotted spoon, transfer the chicken to a plate. Set aside.

2. In a large pot of boiling water, cook the orzo until tender. Drain well.

3. Meanwhile, add the onion to the Dutch oven and cook, stirring frequently, until lightly golden, about 5 minutes. Add the apple and cook, stirring frequently, until slightly softened, about 4 minutes. Stir in the tomato, broth, mint, vinegar, cinnamon, and the remaining ¼ teaspoon salt. Bring to a boil, return the chicken to the pan, and reduce to a simmer. Cover and cook until the chicken is cooked through, about 8 minutes. Divide the orzo among 4 bowls, spoon the chicken mixture alongside, and serve.

Helpful hint: You can make the chicken and sauce up to 8 hours in advance and keep it covered in the refrigerator. Gently reheat it over low heat while you make the orzo. If the mixture is dry, add a little more chicken broth before you reheat it.

FAT: 6G/13%
CALORIES: 430
SATURATED FAT: 1G
CARBOHYDRATE: 58G
PROTEIN: 35G
CHOLESTEROL: 65MG
SODIUM: 435MG

A Greek "kota kapama" is prepared by braising lemon-rubbed chicken in cinnamon-spiced tomato sauce. We've used a touch of wine vinegar in place of the lemon, and added chunks of tart green apple. In traditional fashion, the stew is served with orzo, but rice or mashed potatoes would also be suitable side dishes.

Replete with chicken breasts, turkey sausage, and kidney beans, and served with brown rice, here's a protein-rich meal that's low in fat: The perfect pick-me-up after a strenuous day. It may be hard to believe that this hearty, rich-tasting recipe calls for just one teaspoon of oil.

CHICKEN STEW WITH HOT SAUSAGE

SERVES: 4
WORKING TIME: 25 MINUTES
TOTAL TIME: 45 MINUTES

1 cup brown rice

¼ teaspoon salt

1 teaspoon olive oil

3 ounces hot Italian-style turkey sausage, casings removed

¾ pound skinless, boneless chicken breasts, cut into 1-inch chunks

2 cloves garlic, minced

2 cups thinly sliced leeks (see tip)

1½ cups finely diced red bell pepper

1 cup reduced-sodium beef broth

¼ cup dry sherry or dry white wine

2 teaspoons Worcestershire sauce

15-ounce can pinto beans, rinsed and drained

2 teaspoons cornstarch mixed with 1 tablespoon water

1. In a medium saucepan, bring 2¼ cups of water to a boil. Add the rice and salt, reduce to a simmer, cover, and cook until the rice is tender, about 40 minutes.

2. Meanwhile, in a nonstick Dutch oven or flameproof casserole, heat the oil until hot but not smoking over medium heat. Add the sausage and chicken and cook, breaking up the sausage meat with a spoon, until the chicken is golden brown all over, about 3 minutes. With a slotted spoon, transfer the chicken and sausage to a plate. Set aside.

3. Add the garlic, leeks, and bell pepper to the pan and cook, stirring, until the vegetables are softened, about 8 minutes. Add the broth, sherry, and Worcestershire sauce; return the chicken and sausage to the pan, bring to a boil, and cook until the chicken is cooked through, about 10 minutes. Add the beans and cornstarch mixture and cook, stirring constantly, until slightly thickened, about 2 minutes. Serve with the brown rice.

Helpful hints: To prepare the sausage for this recipe, slit the casing lengthwise with a sharp knife, then peel off the casing with your fingers. The nutlike flavor of brown rice goes well with this stew, but if you're in a hurry, you can substitute the same amount of white rice and cut about 20 minutes from the cooking time in step 1.

FAT: 7G/14%
CALORIES: 445
SATURATED FAT: 1.4G
CARBOHYDRATE: 59G
PROTEIN: 33G
CHOLESTEROL: 61MG
SODIUM: 700MG

TIP

When a recipe calls for leeks to be sliced or diced, first trim the root end and the dark green leaves, then cut the leeks as directed. Place the cut leeks in a bowl of tepid water, let them sit for 1 to 2 minutes, then lift the leeks out of the water, leaving any dirt and grit behind in the bowl. This is easier and faster than splitting and washing whole leeks before slicing them.

DRUNKEN CHICKEN

SERVES: 4
WORKING TIME: 25 MINUTES
TOTAL TIME: 40 MINUTES

You can't blame this chicken for being a bit tipsy—it's been cooked in beer. Because the sauce simmers in an uncovered pot, most of the alcohol will cook off, leaving behind only a rich, malty taste. We suggest dark or amber beer for its robust flavor, but any kind of beer (including alcohol-free) will do. Serve with a salad to complete the meal.

3 tablespoons flour

¾ teaspoon salt

¾ pound skinless, boneless chicken thighs, cut into 1-inch chunks

14½-ounce can no-salt-added stewed tomatoes, drained, juice reserved

2 teaspoons olive oil

1 onion, coarsely chopped

3 cloves garlic, minced

2 teaspoons chili powder

1½ teaspoons ground cumin

¾ teaspoon dried oregano

1 cup dark or amber beer

2 zucchini, halved lengthwise and thinly sliced

15-ounce can red kidney beans, rinsed and drained

1 cup frozen corn kernels

2 teaspoons honey

¼ teaspoon freshly ground black pepper

1. On a sheet of waxed paper, combine the flour and salt. Dredge the chicken in the flour mixture, reserving the excess. In a small bowl, combine the reserved flour mixture with the stewed tomato juice. Set aside.

2. In a nonstick Dutch oven or flameproof casserole, heat the oil until hot but not smoking over medium heat. Add the onion and cook until slightly softened, about 3 minutes. Push the onion to one side of the pan, add the chicken, and cook until golden brown all over, about 8 minutes.

3. Stir in the garlic, chili powder, cumin, and oregano and cook, stirring, until fragrant, about 1 minute. Add the beer and zucchini, bring to a boil, and cook for 5 minutes to reduce slightly. Stir in the reserved flour mixture along with the tomatoes, beans, corn, honey, and pepper. Bring to a simmer and cook until the sauce is slightly thickened and the chicken is cooked through, about 7 minutes. Divide the mixture among 4 bowls and serve.

Helpful hint: You can substitute the same amount of black beans for the red kidney beans if you like.

FAT: 7G/18%
CALORIES: 355
SATURATED FAT: 1.3G
CARBOHYDRATE: 45G
PROTEIN: 27G
CHOLESTEROL: 71MG
SODIUM: 658MG

PROVENÇAL TURKEY SOUP

SERVES: 4
WORKING TIME: 20 MINUTES
TOTAL TIME: 35 MINUTES

2 teaspoons olive oil

1 large onion, coarsely chopped

3 cloves garlic, minced

1 red bell pepper, cut into
1-inch squares

1 yellow summer squash, halved
lengthwise and cut into ½-inch-
thick slices

1 zucchini, halved lengthwise
and cut into ½-inch-thick slices

14½-ounce can no-salt-added
stewed tomatoes, chopped with
their juices

2 cups reduced-sodium chicken
broth, defatted

½ cup chopped fresh basil

¾ teaspoon dried tarragon

¼ teaspoon salt

¾ cup ditalini or other small
pasta shape (3 ounces)

¾ pound skinless, boneless turkey
breast, cut into 1-inch cubes

1. In a nonstick Dutch oven or flameproof casserole, heat the oil
until hot but not smoking over medium heat. Add the onion and
garlic and cook, stirring frequently, until the onion is tender, about
5 minutes. Add the bell pepper and cook, stirring occasionally,
until crisp-tender, about 4 minutes.

2. Add the yellow squash and zucchini and cook for 1 minute, stirring to coat. Add the tomatoes and their juices, the broth, 2 cups
of water, the basil, tarragon, and salt and bring to a boil. Stir in
the pasta and cook, covered, until the pasta is almost tender, about
8 minutes. Add the turkey, cover, and cook until the turkey is
cooked through, about 4 minutes.

*Helpful hint: Make a double batch of the soup and freeze the leftovers in
single portions. Reheat one in the microwave whenever you want a
quick, delicious lunch-for-one.*

FAT: 4G/13%
CALORIES: 279
SATURATED FAT: 0.6G
CARBOHYDRATE: 34G
PROTEIN: 29G
CHOLESTEROL: 53MG
SODIUM: 524MG

28

Brilliant
color is a feature that
many Provençal meals
have in common:
Dishes that originate
in the sun-washed
south of France seem to
radiate a bit of that
sunshine no matter
where they're made.
Thanks to brief
cooking, the red,
yellow, and green
vegetables in this soup
retain their lively hue
and a handful of fresh
basil ensures that the
flavor is as bright as
the color.

Who's afraid of a little garlic? Nobody should be, when the cloves simmer for 15 minutes and are then puréed into a sensuously scented seasoning. In this recipe, the garlic purée takes the place of high-fat flavorings like salt pork or bacon. The soup gets a last-minute toss of fresh parsley— a traditional counterpoint and "antidote" to garlic.

HEARTY CHICKEN AND GARLIC SOUP

SERVES: 4
WORKING TIME: 20 MINUTES
TOTAL TIME: 50 MINUTES

2 cups reduced-sodium chicken broth, defatted

2 whole chicken legs (about 1 pound total), split into drumsticks and thighs (see tip) and skinned

12 cloves garlic, peeled

1½ cups no-salt-added canned tomatoes, drained and chopped

2 large carrots, halved lengthwise and thinly sliced

¾ teaspoon dried thyme

½ teaspoon salt

¼ teaspoon freshly ground black pepper

½ cup long-grain rice

¼ cup chopped fresh parsley

1. In a Dutch oven or flameproof casserole, combine the broth and 4 cups of water. Bring to a boil, add the chicken and garlic, reduce to a simmer, cover, and cook until the chicken is cooked through, about 15 minutes. Transfer the chicken to a cutting board and when cool enough to handle, remove the meat from the bones and cut into small dice. With a slotted spoon, transfer the garlic to a food processor or blender along with ¼ cup of the broth and purée until smooth.

2. Add the garlic purée to the broth in the Dutch oven along with the tomatoes, carrots, thyme, salt, and pepper. Bring to a boil, stir in the rice, reduce to a simmer, cover, and cook until the rice is tender, about 15 minutes. Return the chicken to the pan along with the parsley and cook just until heated through, about 1 minute. Divide the soup among 4 bowls and serve.

Helpful hint: For a slight change of flavor, you can make the soup with parsnips instead of carrots, or you can use one parsnip and one carrot of roughly equal size.

FAT: 3G/12%
CALORIES: 226
SATURATED FAT: 0.7G
CARBOHYDRATE: 32G
PROTEIN: 18G
CHOLESTEROL: 52MG
SODIUM: 685MG

TIP

To split a whole chicken leg, slightly stretch the drumstick and thigh apart to find the ball joint and, with a sharp boning knife, cleanly cut through the joint. Grasping the leg at opposite ends, pull apart the thigh and drumstick.

ASIAN POTTED CHICKEN

SERVES: 4
WORKING TIME: 25 MINUTES
TOTAL TIME: 30 MINUTES

Here's a tangy Asian version of chicken stew: Marinated chicken is simmered with stir-fried vegetables and served over pasta.

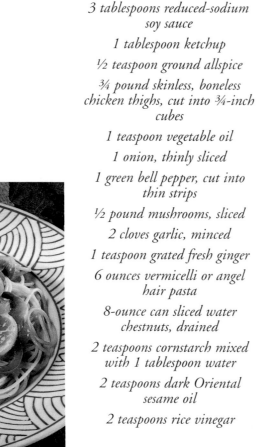

3 tablespoons orange marmalade

3 tablespoons reduced-sodium soy sauce

1 tablespoon ketchup

½ teaspoon ground allspice

¾ pound skinless, boneless chicken thighs, cut into ¾-inch cubes

1 teaspoon vegetable oil

1 onion, thinly sliced

1 green bell pepper, cut into thin strips

½ pound mushrooms, sliced

2 cloves garlic, minced

1 teaspoon grated fresh ginger

6 ounces vermicelli or angel hair pasta

8-ounce can sliced water chestnuts, drained

2 teaspoons cornstarch mixed with 1 tablespoon water

2 teaspoons dark Oriental sesame oil

2 teaspoons rice vinegar

1. In a small bowl, combine the marmalade, soy sauce, ketchup, and allspice. Add the chicken, tossing to coat well. Set aside to marinate while you cook the pasta and vegetables.

2. In a nonstick Dutch oven or large saucepan, heat the vegetable oil until hot but not smoking over medium heat. Add the onion and bell pepper and cook, stirring, until the vegetables are softened, about 4 minutes. Add the mushrooms, garlic, and ginger and cook, stirring, until the mushrooms are tender, about 4 minutes.

3. Meanwhile, in a large pot of boiling water, cook the pasta until just tender. Drain well.

4. Stir the chicken and its marinade into the Dutch oven, bring to a simmer, and cook, stirring, until the chicken is cooked through, about 3 minutes. Stir in the water chestnuts, cornstarch mixture, and ¾ cup of water. Bring to a simmer and cook, stirring, until the sauce is slightly thickened, about 1 minute. Stir in the sesame oil and vinegar. Divide the pasta among 4 plates, spoon the chicken mixture over, and serve.

Helpful hint: Be careful not to overcook the pasta. Both vermicelli and angel hair pasta cook very quickly—the latter in 5 minutes or less.

FAT: 8G/18%
CALORIES: 398
SATURATED FAT: 1.4G
CARBOHYDRATE: 58G
PROTEIN: 25G
CHOLESTEROL: 71MG
SODIUM: 587MG

Turkey Pot au Feu

Serves: 6
Working time: 15 minutes
Total time: 40 minutes

2 cups reduced-sodium chicken broth, defatted

1 teaspoon dried marjoram

¾ teaspoon freshly ground black pepper

¾ teaspoon ground ginger

½ teaspoon salt

3 large carrots, cut into 1-inch pieces

3 parsnips, peeled and cut into 1-inch pieces

1 pound all-purpose potatoes, peeled and cut into 1-inch cubes

2 leeks, cut into 1-inch chunks

½ pound turnips, peeled and cut into 1-inch cubes

1¾ pounds skinless, boneless turkey breast in one piece

⅓ cup chopped fresh parsley

1. In a Dutch oven or flameproof casserole, combine the broth, 5 cups of water, the marjoram, pepper, ginger, and salt and bring to a boil over medium heat. Add the carrots, parsnips, potatoes, leeks, and turnips and return to a boil. Add the turkey, reduce the heat to a simmer, cover, and cook until the vegetables are tender and the turkey is cooked through, about 15 minutes.

2. Transfer the turkey to a cutting board and when cool enough to handle, cut into bite-size pieces. Remove 1 cup of the vegetables, transfer to a food processor, and process to a smooth purée. Return the turkey and purée to the pot, add the parsley, and bring to a boil. Remove from the heat and serve.

Helpful hints: Parsnips are usually sold in bags or small bunches. Small parsnips—about 8 inches long—will be the most tender; choose firm, fairly smooth ones that taper evenly from top to tip. Instead of transferring the vegetables to a food processor, you can use a hand blender right in the pot of soup. Run the blender in brief on-and-off pulses, stirring often to check consistency, to purée some of the vegetables while leaving the soup chunky.

French cooks present this stew in two courses: first broth, then meat and vegetables. Here, it's served as a single dish.

Fat: 1g/3%
Calories: 296
Saturated Fat: 0.3g
Carbohydrate: 34g
Protein: 37g
Cholesterol: 82mg
Sodium: 518mg

SPICY SWEET POTATO SOUP WITH TURKEY SAUSAGE

SERVES: 4
WORKING TIME: 15 MINUTES
TOTAL TIME: 7 TO 9 HOURS

With a slow cooker in your kitchen, you can serve a stew made from scratch, even if you're out of the house all day. During eight hours of slow simmering, the flavor of the spicy sausage infuses the beans (we've used both black and red) and potatoes with flavor. Make a simple salad while the kids set the table.

½ cup dried black beans, rinsed and picked over

½ cup dried small red chili beans, rinsed and picked over

1½ pounds sweet potatoes, peeled, quartered lengthwise and cut into ¼-inch-thick slices

1 large red bell pepper, cut into ½-inch pieces

4½-ounce can chopped mild green chilies, drained

6 scallions, thinly sliced

6 cloves garlic, minced

2 tablespoons minced fresh ginger

¾ teaspoon dried oregano

¼ teaspoon red pepper flakes

3 tablespoons fresh lime juice

½ pound hot Italian-style turkey sausage, casings removed

¼ teaspoon salt

1. In a medium pot, combine the dried beans with enough water to cover them by 2 inches. Bring to a boil and boil for 2 minutes. Remove from the heat, cover, and let stand for 1 hour. Drain well.

2. In a 4-quart electric slow cooker, combine the soaked beans, sweet potatoes, bell pepper, green chilies, scallions, garlic, ginger, oregano, red pepper flakes, lime juice, sausage, and 3 cups of water. Cover, and with the setting on low, cook until the beans and sweet potatoes are tender, 6 to 8 hours. Stir in the salt, ladle into 4 bowls, and serve.

Helpful hint: To save time in the morning, presoak the beans overnight: Place them in a bowl with water to cover by 2 inches, cover, and refrigerate. The next morning, drain the beans and assemble the stew in the slow cooker.

FAT: 7G/17%
CALORIES: 366
SATURATED FAT: 1.9G
CARBOHYDRATE: 59G
PROTEIN: 20G
CHOLESTEROL: 30MG
SODIUM: 767MG

Out of Morocco comes the wondrous tagine, a sweetly spiced stew of meat, vegetables, and fruit served with couscous. Along with the turkey, we've used winter squash, turnip, apple, and dried fruit. The quick-cooking couscous, which is sold in most supermarkets, is ready in just 5 minutes.

TURKEY TAGINE WITH APRICOTS AND HONEY

SERVES: 4
WORKING TIME: 30 MINUTES
TOTAL TIME: 45 MINUTES

1 cup couscous

1 cup boiling water

¼ cup flour

2 teaspoons paprika

1 teaspoon ground coriander

¾ teaspoon ground cumin

¾ teaspoon salt

½ teaspoon cinnamon

1 pound turkey cutlets, cut crosswise into 1-inch-wide strips

13¾-ounce can reduced-sodium chicken broth, defatted

1 tablespoon olive oil

3 cups cubed butternut squash

1 cup turnip, diced

½ cup dried Turkish apricots (see tip), cut into thin slivers

1 tablespoon white wine vinegar

1 Granny Smith apple, peeled, cored, and cut into ¾-inch cubes

2 tablespoons dried currants

15-ounce can chick-peas, rinsed and drained

1. In a medium heatproof bowl, combine the couscous and boiling water. Let stand until the couscous is tender and the water is absorbed, about 5 minutes.

2. Meanwhile, on a sheet of waxed paper, combine the flour, paprika, coriander, cumin, salt, and cinnamon. Dredge the turkey in the flour mixture, shaking off and reserving the excess. In a small bowl, combine the reserved dredging mixture with the broth. Set aside.

3. In a nonstick Dutch oven or flameproof casserole, heat the oil until hot but not smoking over medium heat. Add the turkey and cook until lightly browned, about 5 minutes. With a slotted spoon, transfer the turkey to a plate. Add the broth-flour mixture to the pan along with the squash, turnip, and apricots. Bring to simmer, cover, and cook, stirring occasionally, until the vegetables are firm-tender, about 10 minutes.

4. Return the turkey to the pan, along with the vinegar, apple, currants, and chick-peas. Simmer until the turkey is cooked through and the apple is softened, about 5 minutes. Divide the couscous among 4 bowls, spoon the turkey mixture over, and serve.

FAT: 7G/11%
CALORIES: 569
SATURATED FAT: 0.9G
CARBOHYDRATE: 86G
PROTEIN: 42G
CHOLESTEROL: 70MG
SODIUM: 886MG

TIP

Dried Turkish apricots (top) are whole, rather than halved; they're plumper and less tart than California apricots (bottom). If using California apricots, soak them in boiling water to cover for 20 minutes before using them in this recipe.

CARIBBEAN CHICKEN STEW

SERVES: 4
WORKING TIME: 25 MINUTES
TOTAL TIME: 40 MINUTES

Here's a refreshing combination of the familiar and the exotic. Red potatoes, sweet potatoes, onion, and tender morsels of chicken serve as the sturdy foundation of this stew; the jazzy notes come from allspice, ginger, lime juice, and banana. In the Caribbean islands, plantains—large, starchy bananas—are used like potatoes.

4 scallions, coarsely chopped, white and green parts kept separate

1 tablespoon firmly packed light brown sugar

2 cloves garlic, minced

1 teaspoon ground ginger

¾ teaspoon dried marjoram

¼ teaspoon ground allspice

¾ pound skinless, boneless chicken thighs, cut into 1-inch cubes

1 teaspoon olive oil

1 cup chopped red onion

13¾-ounce can reduced-sodium chicken broth, defatted

½ pound sweet potatoes, peeled and cut into ½-inch dice

½ pound red potatoes, cut into ½-inch dice

½ teaspoon salt

¼ cup chopped fresh parsley

1 firm-ripe banana, cut into ¾-inch slices

2 teaspoons cornstarch mixed with 1 tablespoon water

1 teaspoon fresh lime juice

1. In a medium bowl, combine the scallion whites, brown sugar, garlic, ginger, marjoram, and allspice. Add the chicken, tossing to coat.

2. In a nonstick Dutch oven or flameproof casserole, heat the oil until hot but not smoking over medium heat. Add the onion and cook until slightly softened, about 2 minutes. Add the chicken and cook until golden brown all over, about 5 minutes.

3. Add the broth, 1 cup of water, the sweet potatoes, red potatoes, and salt to the pan. Bring to a simmer, cover, and cook until the potatoes are just tender, about 8 minutes. Stir in the scallion greens, the parsley, banana, and cornstarch mixture and cook, stirring, until slightly thickened, about 2 minutes. Stir in the lime juice, divide among 4 bowls, and serve.

Helpful hint: To save a little time, heat the broth and water for step 3 while you cook the onion and brown the chicken; the hot liquid will come to a simmer more quickly when you add it to the pot.

FAT: 5G/16%
CALORIES: 278
SATURATED FAT: 1.1G
CARBOHYDRATE: 38G
PROTEIN: 21G
CHOLESTEROL: 71MG
SODIUM: 634MG

SPANISH CHICKEN AND RICE SOUP

SERVES: 4
WORKING TIME: 20 MINUTES
TOTAL TIME: 35 MINUTES

2 cups reduced-sodium chicken
broth, defatted

¼ cup dry sherry or dry white
wine

2 cloves garlic, minced

1½ teaspoons paprika

⅛ teaspoon saffron, or
¼ teaspoon turmeric

½ teaspoon salt

¼ teaspoon freshly ground black
pepper

½ cup long-grain rice

¾ pound skinless, boneless
chicken thighs, cut into 1-inch
cubes

1 green bell pepper, cut into
1-inch squares

1 red bell pepper, cut into
1-inch squares

1 cup frozen peas

1. In a Dutch oven or flameproof casserole, combine the broth,
   3 cups of water, the sherry, garlic, paprika, saffron, salt, and black
   pepper. Bring to a boil over medium heat, add the rice, and cook
   for 5 minutes to blend the flavors.

2. Add the chicken and bell peppers to the pan. Reduce the heat to a
   simmer, cover, and cook until the rice is tender and the chicken is
   cooked through, about 15 minutes. Stir in the peas and cook just
   until the peas are heated through, about 1 minute.

*Helpful hint: The finest and most expensive saffron comes in individual
threads, which should be gently crumbled just before using and then
measured in a measuring spoon. Use the less expensive powdered saffron
as you would any other spice.*

FAT: 4G/14%
CALORIES: 256
SATURATED FAT: 0.9G
CARBOHYDRATE: 28G
PROTEIN: 23G
CHOLESTEROL: 71MG
SODIUM: 713MG

40

Chicken soup with rice is a cold-weather standard, but the basic format could use some added excitement. This soup draws its inspiration from a Spanish paella: Suffused with the uniquely pungent aroma and flavor of saffron, it has golden-yellow rice, chicken, bell peppers, and green peas in a broth redolent of garlic and sherry, the fortified wine that originated in Spain.

While bouillabaisse, a highly seasoned French stew, is usually made with fish, ours is based on turkey rather than seafood. The rouille (pronounced roo-EE) —a spicy mixture stirred into the soup and spread on the croutons—also breaks with tradition: Our low-fat version is thickened with potatoes rather than the usual olive oil and bread crumbs.

TURKEY BOUILLABAISSE

SERVES: 4
WORKING TIME: 20 MINUTES
TOTAL TIME: 35 MINUTES

1 baking potato (8 ounces),
peeled and thinly sliced

2 cloves garlic, peeled, plus
3 cloves garlic, minced

1 cup jarred roasted red peppers,
rinsed and drained

2 tablespoons no-salt-added
tomato paste

¼ teaspoon red pepper flakes

2 teaspoons olive oil

1 fennel bulb (about ¾ pound),
trimmed and cut into ½-inch
slices (see tip)

1 red bell pepper, cut into
1-inch squares

2 tomatoes, coarsely chopped

2 cups reduced-sodium chicken
broth, defatted

¼ cup orange juice

½ teaspoon grated orange zest

½ teaspoon fennel seeds

¼ teaspoon salt

¾ pound turkey cutlets, cut into
½-inch cubes

4 ounces French bread, cut into
12 slices and toasted

1. In a small pot of boiling water, cook the potato until almost tender, about 8 minutes. Add the 2 whole garlic cloves and cook until the potato is tender, about 2 minutes. Drain well. In a food processor, combine the drained potato and garlic, the roasted red peppers, 1 tablespoon of the tomato paste, and the red pepper flakes. Process until just blended but still slightly chunky, about 30 seconds. Set aside.

2. In a nonstick Dutch oven or flameproof casserole, heat the oil until hot but not smoking over medium heat. Add the fennel, bell pepper, and minced garlic and cook, stirring frequently, until the fennel is lightly colored and the pepper is crisp-tender, about 5 minutes. Stir in the tomatoes, broth, orange juice, 2½ cups of water, the orange zest, fennel seeds, the remaining 1 tablespoon tomato paste, and the salt. Bring to a boil, reduce to a simmer, cover, and cook until the flavors have blended, about 7 minutes. Stir in the turkey, cover, and cook just until the turkey is cooked through, about 4 minutes.

3. Stir half of the roasted pepper purée into the soup and cook for 30 seconds to heat through. Spread the remaining roasted pepper purée on the toast. Spoon the soup into 4 soup bowls, place 3 slices of toast in each bowl, and serve.

FAT: 4G/12%
CALORIES: 296
SATURATED FAT: 0.7G
CARBOHYDRATE: 36G
PROTEIN: 28G
CHOLESTEROL: 53MG
SODIUM: 827MG

To prepare fresh fennel, cut the stalks from the bulb, then trim the stem end and any tough outer sections from the bulb. Cut the bulb crosswise into ½-inch slices. If fennel is not available, substitute an equal amount of sliced celery plus an additional ¼ teaspoon fennel seeds.

SWEET AND SPICY CHICKEN STEW

SERVES: 4
WORKING TIME: 20 MINUTES
TOTAL TIME: 40 MINUTES

*H*ere's a stew that starts out resembling a stir-fry: The chicken cubes and diced pepper are skillet-cooked with garlic and scallions before the sweet potato and broth are added. This two-step method results in a very flavorful dish. The seasonings are a delightful blend of sweet and hot, and the broth is delicately thickened with cornstarch.

1 cup long-grain rice
¾ teaspoon salt
2 tablespoons flour
¼ teaspoon freshly ground black pepper
¾ pound skinless, boneless chicken thighs, cut into 2-inch pieces
2 teaspoons olive oil
6 scallions, cut into 1-inch lengths
3 cloves garlic, slivered
1 red bell pepper, diced
1 sweet potato (12 ounces), peeled and cut into 1-inch cubes
2 cups reduced-sodium chicken broth, defatted
¾ teaspoon ground cumin
½ teaspoon ground ginger
½ teaspoon ground cinnamon
¼ teaspoon hot pepper sauce
1 cup frozen peas
1 teaspoon cornstarch mixed with 1 tablespoon water

1. In a medium saucepan, bring 2¼ cups of water to a boil. Add the rice and ¼ teaspoon of the salt, reduce to a simmer, cover, and cook until the rice is tender, about 17 minutes.

2. Meanwhile, on a sheet of waxed paper, combine the the flour, ¼ teaspoon of the salt, and the black pepper. Dredge the chicken in the flour mixture, shaking off the excess. In a large nonstick skillet, heat the oil until hot but not smoking over medium heat. Add the chicken and cook until golden brown, about 3 minutes per side. With a slotted spoon, transfer the chicken to a plate.

3. Add the scallions and garlic to the pan and cook, stirring occasionally, until the scallions are softened, about 2 minutes. Add the bell pepper and cook, stirring occasionally, until crisp-tender, about 4 minutes. Add the sweet potato, stirring to coat. Add the broth, cumin, ginger, cinnamon, hot pepper sauce, and the remaining ¼ teaspoon salt. Bring to a boil, reduce to a simmer, cover, and cook, stirring occasionally, until the sweet potato is firm-tender, about 5 minutes.

4. Return the chicken to the skillet and cook until the chicken is cooked through, about 5 minutes. Bring to a boil, stir in the peas and cornstarch mixture and cook, stirring constantly, until the mixture is slightly thickened, about 1 minute. Divide among 4 bowls, spoon the rice alongside, and serve.

FAT: 6G/13%
CALORIES: 426
SATURATED FAT: 1.3G
CARBOHYDRATE: 65G
PROTEIN: 26G
CHOLESTEROL: 71MG
SODIUM: 871MG

Hearty Turkey and Rice Soup

Serves: 4
Working Time: 25 minutes
Total Time: 40 minutes

This brimming bowl of turkey, rice, and vegetable soup contains no heavy cream—but it sure tastes like a cream soup to us.

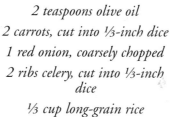

2 teaspoons olive oil

2 carrots, cut into ⅓-inch dice

1 red onion, coarsely chopped

2 ribs celery, cut into ⅓-inch dice

⅓ cup long-grain rice

¾ teaspoon dried sage

13¾-ounce can reduced-sodium chicken broth, defatted

¾ teaspoon salt

¾ pound turkey cutlets, cut into 2 x ¾-inch strips

1 zucchini, cut into ⅓-inch dice

1 cup frozen peas

1 tablespoon grated fresh ginger

1 cup evaporated skimmed milk

1 tablespoon cornstarch

¼ cup reduced-fat sour cream

1. In a nonstick Dutch oven or flameproof casserole, heat the oil until hot but not smoking over medium-high heat. Add the carrots, onion, and celery and cook until the vegetables are softened, about 4 minutes. Stir in the rice and sage and cook, stirring to coat the rice. Add the broth, 1 cup of water, and the salt; bring to a simmer and cook until the rice is tender, about 15 minutes.

2. Stir in the turkey, zucchini, peas, and ginger. Bring to a boil, reduce the heat to a simmer, and cook until the turkey is cooked through, about 5 minutes.

3. Meanwhile, in a small bowl, combine the evaporated milk and cornstarch. Stir the cornstarch mixture into the soup and cook, stirring constantly, until slightly thickened, about 2 minutes. Remove from the heat and stir in the sour cream. Divide among 4 bowls and serve.

Helpful hint: This soup can be partially prepared in advance. Complete step 1, cover, and refrigerate. At serving time, return the soup to the stovetop and continue with step 2 and the rest of the recipe.

Fat: 5g/14%
Calories: 331
Saturated Fat: 1.6g
Carbohydrate: 38g
Protein: 33g
Cholesterol: 60mg
Sodium: 880mg

BEEF, PORK & LAMB

2

LAMB AND BARLEY SOUP

SERVES: 4
WORKING TIME: 30 MINUTES
TOTAL TIME: 50 MINUTES

Barley, one of the world's first domesticated crops, may qualify as the original comfort food. A simmering pot of barley soup—especially one made with savory lamb, garlic, and pungent rosemary—fills the kitchen with an enticing fragrance, piquing the appetite of anyone within range. A salad with a tart citrus dressing would be a pleasant contrast to the richness of the stew.

1 teaspoon olive oil
1 onion, coarsely diced
3 cloves garlic, minced
3 carrots, thinly sliced
10 ounces well-trimmed lamb shoulder, cut into bite-size pieces
2 tomatoes, coarsely chopped
1 large baking potato (8 ounces), peeled and cut into ½-inch dice
1 large turnip (6 ounces), peeled and cut into ½-inch dice
½ teaspoon dried rosemary
½ teaspoon ground ginger
¾ teaspoon salt
⅔ cup quick-cooking barley

1. In a nonstick Dutch oven, heat the oil until hot but not smoking over medium heat. Add the onion and garlic and cook, stirring frequently, until the onion is lightly browned, about 7 minutes. Add the carrots and cook, stirring frequently, until crisp-tender, about 4 minutes.

2. Add the lamb and cook until no longer pink, about 3 minutes. Stir in the tomatoes, potato, turnip, rosemary, ginger, salt, and 5 cups of water and bring to a boil. Add the barley, reduce the heat to a simmer, cover, and cook until the barley is tender, about 15 minutes.

Helpful hint: Lamb shoulder is great for soups and stews; slow-cooking brings out its excellent flavor and softens this somewhat tough cut. Be sure to get boneless shoulder for this recipe.

FAT: 7G/21%
CALORIES: 303
SATURATED FAT: 1.9G
CARBOHYDRATE: 42G
PROTEIN: 20G
CHOLESTEROL: 47MG
SODIUM: 514MG

Cannellini Soup with Pork Meatballs

SERVES: 4
WORKING TIME: 25 MINUTES
TOTAL TIME: 45 MINUTES

You'll think you're dining in a Tuscan village when you sit down to this delightfully different soup. The light tomato broth is the backdrop for two favorite Tuscan ingredients: kale and cannellini (white kidney beans). And the pork meatballs are redolent of sage, one of Tuscany's most beloved herbs. Where an Italian cook would use pepperoncini, we've substituted a pickled jalapeño.

2 slices (1 ounce each) white sandwich bread

¼ cup low-fat (1%) milk

½ pound lean ground pork

3 cloves garlic, minced

½ teaspoon dried oregano or marjoram

¼ teaspoon dried sage

¼ teaspoon salt

2 teaspoons olive oil

1 red bell pepper, diced

1 green bell pepper, diced

1 pickled jalapeño pepper, seeded and minced

19-ounce can white kidney beans (cannellini), rinsed and drained

2 cups reduced-sodium chicken broth, defatted

1 cup low-sodium tomato-vegetable juice

4 cups shredded kale or spinach

1. Tear the bread into small pieces and place in a medium bowl. Pour the milk over the bread, mixing to combine. Add the pork, garlic, oregano, sage, and salt and mix well. Form into 24 small meatballs. Set aside.

2. In a Dutch oven or large saucepan, heat the oil until hot but not smoking over medium heat. Add the bell peppers and jalapeño and cook, stirring frequently, until the bell peppers are crisp-tender, about 5 minutes. Add the beans, stirring to coat. Add the broth, tomato-vegetable juice, and 3 cups of water and bring to a boil over medium heat. Reduce to a simmer, cover, and cook for 5 minutes to blend the flavors.

3. Add the meatballs and kale, cover, and cook until the meatballs are cooked through and the kale is tender, about 5 minutes. Ladle the soup into 4 bowls and serve.

Helpful hint: Remember that whenever you need to form ground meat into a shape—for burgers, meat loaf, or meatballs—the more gently you handle the mixture, the more tender the finished product will be.

FAT: 9G/25%
CALORIES: 319
SATURATED FAT: 2.2G
CARBOHYDRATE: 36G
PROTEIN: 24G
CHOLESTEROL: 39MG
SODIUM: 881MG

If you've ever aspired to master the French culinary classics, you've probably made boeuf à la bourguignonne. Traditional recipes call for salt pork or fatty bacon, but we've updated the wine-sauced beef stew so that you need only a few teaspoons of oil; we've also substituted frozen pearl onions for fresh to save you a nice chunk of time.

BEEF BURGUNDY

SERVES: 4
WORKING TIME: 25 MINUTES
TOTAL TIME: 40 MINUTES

2 tablespoons flour

½ teaspoon salt

½ teaspoon freshly ground black pepper

¾ pound well-trimmed bottom round of beef, cut into ¾-inch cubes

2 teaspoons olive oil

1½ cups frozen pearl onions

6 cloves garlic, peeled and halved

3 carrots, halved lengthwise and cut into 1-inch pieces

¾ pound small mushrooms

1 cup dry red wine

⅔ cup reduced-sodium beef broth

2 tablespoons no-salt-added tomato paste

Three 3 x ½-inch strips of orange zest (see tip)

½ teaspoon dried thyme

1 bay leaf

1 zucchini, halved lengthwise and thinly sliced

¼ cup chopped fresh parsley

1. On a sheet of waxed paper, combine the flour, ¼ teaspoon of the salt, and ¼ teaspoon of the pepper. Dredge the beef in the flour mixture, shaking off and reserving the excess.

2. In a nonstick Dutch oven or flameproof casserole, heat the oil until hot but not smoking over medium heat. Add the beef and cook until golden brown, about 4 minutes. With a slotted spoon, transfer the beef to a plate. Set aside.

3. Add the pearl onions and garlic to the pan and cook, stirring frequently, until golden, about 2 minutes. Add the carrots and mushrooms and cook, stirring frequently, until lightly colored, about 4 minutes. Add the wine, increase the heat to high, and cook until reduced by half, about 3 minutes. Stir in the broth, tomato paste, orange zest, thyme, bay leaf, and the remaining ¼ teaspoon salt and remaining ¼ teaspoon pepper. Bring to a boil, reduce to a simmer, cover, and cook until the vegetables are tender, about 8 minutes.

4. In a small bowl, stir together the reserved dredging mixture and ⅓ cup of water. Stir the flour mixture into the pan, bring to a boil, and cook, stirring, until slightly thickened, about 3 minutes. Return the beef to the pan, add the zucchini, and simmer gently until the beef is just cooked through, about 2 minutes. Discard the orange zest and bay leaf. Stir in the parsley, divide the mixture among 4 bowls, and serve.

FAT: 8G/24%
CALORIES: 296
SATURATED FAT: 2G
CARBOHYDRATE: 25G
PROTEIN: 24G
CHOLESTEROL: 50MG
SODIUM: 469MG

TIP

To remove a strip of zest from an orange, use a swivel-bladed vegetable peeler to cut off a piece of the outer colored rind, avoiding the bitter white pith underneath. The zest contains the intensely flavored oil found in the skin.

OLD-FASHIONED VEGETABLE-BEEF SOUP

SERVES: 4
WORKING TIME: 15 MINUTES
TOTAL TIME: 30 MINUTES

2 cups reduced-sodium beef
broth
1 tomato, coarsely chopped
3 cloves garlic, minced
½ teaspoon dried thyme
½ teaspoon dried rosemary
½ teaspoon Worcestershire sauce
¼ teaspoon salt
4 ounces elbow macaroni
1 cup frozen baby lima beans
¾ pound well-trimmed top
round of beef, cut into ½-inch
dice
1 cup frozen corn kernels
3 tablespoons ketchup

1. In a Dutch oven or large saucepan, combine the broth, tomato, garlic, thyme, rosemary, Worcestershire sauce, salt, and 3 cups of water. Bring to a boil over medium heat, cover, and cook for 5 minutes to blend the flavors.

2. Stir in the macaroni and lima beans, cover, and cook for 5 minutes. Stir in the beef, corn, and ketchup, cover, and cook until the meat is cooked through and the macaroni is tender, about 5 minutes.

Helpful hint: Worcestershire sauce "beefs up" soups and stews with a complex blend of ingredients that includes anchovies, soy sauce, molasses, garlic, onions, and vinegar.

FAT: 4G/11%
CALORIES: 337
SATURATED FAT: 1.1G
CARBOHYDRATE: 46G
PROTEIN: 30G
CHOLESTEROL: 49MG
SODIUM: 657MG

You'll find row upon row of soup cans labeled "old-fashioned" on your supermarket's shelves, but we think you'll be much happier with this recipe, which uses fresh beef, tomato, and garlic for maximum flavor, and frozen corn and lima beans for convenience. You might want to double the recipe so your family can enjoy the soup as a take-along lunch later in the week.

MEXICAN-STYLE BEEF STEW

SERVES: 4
WORKING TIME: 30 MINUTES
TOTAL TIME: 45 MINUTES

This eye-catching stew bears a certain resemblance to chili, but chick-peas and green peas take the place of beans. And rather than blazing with the heat of chili powder, this stew glows with the vibrant flavors of cumin, oregano, and turmeric. The green chilies add a little heat, but there is nothing here to intimidate those with tender palates.

1 teaspoon ground cumin

1 teaspoon dried oregano

½ teaspoon freshly ground black pepper

½ teaspoon salt

2 tablespoons flour

¾ pound well-trimmed top round of beef, cut into 1-inch cubes

1 tablespoon olive oil

1 large onion, coarsely chopped

3 cloves garlic, slivered

2 red bell peppers, cut into 1-inch squares

4½-ounce can chopped mild green chilies, drained

½ teaspoon turmeric

⅔ cup reduced-sodium chicken broth, defatted

19-ounce can chick-peas, rinsed and drained

1 cup frozen peas

2 tablespoons fresh lemon juice

¼ cup chopped fresh parsley

1. On a sheet of waxed paper, combine ½ teaspoon of the cumin, ½ teaspoon of the oregano, ¼ teaspoon of the black pepper, and ¼ teaspoon of the salt. Place the flour on a second sheet of wax paper. Add the beef to the spice mixture, rubbing the mixture into the meat. Dredge the beef in the flour, shaking off the excess.

2. In a Dutch oven or large saucepan, heat 2 teaspoons of the oil until hot but not smoking over medium heat. Add the beef and cook until lightly browned, about 4 minutes. With a slotted spoon, transfer the beef to a plate. Set aside.

3. Add the remaining 1 teaspoon oil to the pan along with the onion and garlic and cook, stirring frequently, until the onion is softened, about 5 minutes. Add the bell peppers and cook, stirring frequently, until crisp-tender, about 4 minutes. Add the green chilies, turmeric, and the remaining ½ teaspoon cumin, ½ teaspoon oregano, ¼ teaspoon black pepper, and ¼ teaspoon salt, stirring to combine. Add the broth, bring to a boil, and stir in the chick-peas. Reduce to a simmer, cover, and cook for 10 minutes to blend the flavors.

4. Return the beef to the pan along with the peas and cook just until the beef is cooked through and the peas are hot, about 3 minutes. Stir in the lemon juice and parsley and serve.

FAT: 9G/25%
CALORIES: 325
SATURATED FAT: 1.5G
CARBOHYDRATE: 33G
PROTEIN: 29G
CHOLESTEROL: 49MG
SODIUM: 815MG

HEARTY BEEF AND VEGETABLE STEW

SERVES: 4
WORKING TIME: 30 MINUTES
TOTAL TIME: 55 MINUTES

This outstanding stew brims with hefty cubes of beef, carrots, red potatoes, and rutabaga. Puréed vegetables thicken the broth.

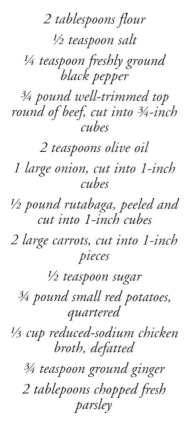

2 tablespoons flour

½ teaspoon salt

¼ teaspoon freshly ground black pepper

¾ pound well-trimmed top round of beef, cut into ¾-inch cubes

2 teaspoons olive oil

1 large onion, cut into 1-inch cubes

½ pound rutabaga, peeled and cut into 1-inch cubes

2 large carrots, cut into 1-inch pieces

½ teaspoon sugar

¾ pound small red potatoes, quartered

⅓ cup reduced-sodium chicken broth, defatted

¾ teaspoon ground ginger

2 tablepoons chopped fresh parsley

1. On a sheet of waxed paper, combine the flour, ¼ teaspoon of the salt, and the pepper. Dredge the beef in the flour mixture, shaking off the excess.

2. In a Dutch oven or flameproof casserole, heat the oil until hot but not smoking over medium heat. Add the beef and cook until lightly browned, about 4 minutes. With a slotted spoon, transfer the beef to a plate. Add the onion, rutabaga, and carrots to the pan, sprinkle the sugar on top, and cook, stirring frequently, until the vegetables are lightly browned, about 4 minutes.

3. Add the potatoes, broth, 1 cup of water, the ginger, and remaining ¼ teaspoon salt and bring to a boil. Reduce to a simmer, cover, and cook until the vegetables are firm-tender, about 20 minutes. With a slotted spoon, transfer ½ cup of the vegetables to a food processor. Add ¼ cup of the cooking liquid and process to a coarse purée. Stir the purée into the stew, return the beef to the pan, and simmer, uncovered, until the beef is just cooked through, about 2 minutes. Divide the stew among 4 bowls, sprinkle with the parsley, and serve.

Helpful hint: Instead of transferring the vegetables to a food processor, you can use a hand blender right in the pot. Run the blender in 1 or 2 on-and-off pulses to purée about a ½ cup of the vegetables, while leaving the stew chunky.

FAT: 6G/20%
CALORIES: 277
SATURATED FAT: 1.3G
CARBOHYDRATE: 33G
PROTEIN: 24G
CHOLESTEROL: 49MG
SODIUM: 407MG

Beef, Bean, and Butternut Soup

Serves: 4
Working time: 25 minutes
Total time: 40 minutes

2 teaspoons olive oil

1 red onion, cut into ½-inch cubes

3 cloves garlic, minced

1¼ pounds butternut squash, peeled and cut into 1-inch cubes

2 teaspoons sugar

2 tablespoons red wine vinegar

⅓ cup chopped fresh mint

½ teaspoon dried oregano

2 cups reduced-sodium beef broth

16-ounce can pinto beans, rinsed and drained

10 ounces well-trimmed top round of beef, cut into bite-size pieces

1 zucchini, quartered lengthwise and thinly sliced

1. In a nonstick Dutch oven or flameproof casserole, heat the oil until hot but not smoking over medium heat. Add the onion and garlic and cook, stirring frequently, until the onion is softened, about 5 minutes. Add the butternut squash, sprinkle with the sugar and cook, stirring frequently, until the squash is lightly browned, about 5 minutes.

2. Add the vinegar, mint, and oregano to the pan, stirring to coat. Add the broth and 3 cups of water and bring to a boil. Stir in the beans and beef, cover, and simmer until the squash is tender, about 10 minutes. Stir in the zucchini, cover, and cook just until the zucchini is tender and the meat is cooked through, about 5 minutes. Ladle the soup into 4 bowls and serve.

Helpful hint: A butternut squash can range in weight from about 2 to 4 pounds. If you have any squash left over, you can turn it into a delicious side dish for meat or poultry: Cut the squash into large chunks (you do not need to peel them), sprinkle with some brown sugar or drizzle with maple syrup, and bake at 350° for 15 to 25 minutes.

Fat: 5g/16%
Calories: 279
Saturated Fat: 1.2g
Carbohydrate: 34g
Protein: 25g
Cholesterol: 40mg
Sodium: 542mg

Winter squash is cooked with a little sugar, then balanced with a splash of wine vinegar for this tangy-sweet soup.

HUNGARIAN BEEF, TOMATO, AND RICE SOUP

SERVES: 4
WORKING TIME: 25 MINUTES
TOTAL TIME: 45 MINUTES

Hungarian cooks use the fine paprika produced in their country to color and season such dishes as chicken paprikash and their world-renowned goulash. Here, paprika adds its singular flavor to a rosy dilled soup served with a dollop of sour cream—a typically Hungarian touch. Offer a crisp salad alongside as a refreshing contrast to the soup's intense flavors.

2 teaspoons olive oil
1 large onion, coarsely diced
2 carrots, halved lengthwise and thinly sliced
2 teaspoons sugar
2 teaspoons paprika
1 tomato, coarsely chopped
8-ounce can no-salt-added tomato sauce
1½ cups reduced-sodium beef broth
½ cup snipped fresh dill
2 tablespoons red wine vinegar
¾ teaspoon salt
½ cup long-grain rice
10 ounces well-trimmed top round of beef, cut into ¼-inch dice
¼ cup reduced-fat sour cream

1. In a Dutch oven or flameproof casserole, heat the oil until hot but not smoking over medium heat. Add the onion and cook, stirring frequently, until lightly browned, about 7 minutes. Add the carrots and cook, stirring frequently, until crisp-tender, about 3 minutes. Sprinkle the sugar over the vegetables, increase the heat to high, and cook, stirring constantly, until the carrots are lightly browned, about 2 minutes. Add the paprika and cook for 30 seconds, stirring to coat.

2. Add the tomato, tomato sauce, broth, 3 cups of water, ¼ cup of the dill, the vinegar, and salt to the pan and bring to a boil. Add the rice, cover, reduce to a simmer, and cook until the rice is tender, about 15 minutes.

3. Stir in the beef and cook until just cooked through, about 3 minutes. Ladle into 4 soup bowls, top each bowl with 1 tablespoon of the sour cream and 1 tablespoon of the remaining dill, and serve.

Helpful hint: If you can't get a nice fresh tomato, substitute two canned plum tomatoes, drained and coarsely chopped.

FAT: 7G/21%
CALORIES: 307
SATURATED FAT: 2.2G
CARBOHYDRATE: 38G
PROTEIN: 23G
CHOLESTEROL: 45MG
SODIUM: 723MG

BEEF GUMBO

SERVES: 4
WORKING TIME: 15 MINUTES
TOTAL TIME: 35 MINUTES

The word gumbo comes from an African word, "quingumbo," which means okra. Gumbos are thickened either with okra (which releases a thickening substance as it cooks) or with filé powder, which is made from sassafras leaves. We've boosted the texture of this Louisiana classic with tapioca, a starch derived from cassava roots.

1 teaspoon olive oil

3 tablespoons coarsely chopped Canadian bacon (1 ounce)

4 scallions, thinly sliced

1 green bell pepper, cut into 1-inch squares

2 cloves garlic, minced

14½-ounce can no-salt-added stewed tomatoes, chopped with their juices

2 cups reduced-sodium beef broth

2 teaspoons chili powder

¾ teaspoon dried thyme

¾ teaspoon dried oregano

½ teaspoon salt

10-ounce package frozen cut okra

1 tablespoon minute tapioca

10 ounces well-trimmed top round of beef, cut into bite-size pieces

1½ cups frozen corn kernels

1. In a nonstick Dutch oven or flameproof casserole, heat the oil until hot but not smoking over medium heat. Add the Canadian bacon, scallions, bell pepper, and garlic and cook, stirring frequently, until the vegetables are softened, about 5 minutes.

2. Stir in the tomatoes and their juices, the broth, 3 cups of water, the chili powder, thyme, oregano, and salt. Bring to a boil, reduce to a simmer, cover, and cook for 5 minutes to blend the flavors. Add the okra, cover, and cook until the okra is tender, about 10 minutes.

3. Meanwhile, place the tapioca in a small bowl and stir in ½ cup of the simmering broth; let stand for 5 minutes to soften. Stir the tapioca mixture, beef, and corn into the soup and cook, uncovered, until the soup is slightly thickened and the beef is just cooked through, about 5 minutes. Ladle the soup into 4 bowls and serve.

Helpful hint: A very effective thickener for soups and sauces, tapioca comes in powder, flake, bead, and granule form. Minute tapioca is the quick-cooking granular form of this useful ingredient.

FAT: 5G/18%
CALORIES: 251
SATURATED FAT: 1.2G
CARBOHYDRATE: 31G
PROTEIN: 24G
CHOLESTEROL: 44MG
SODIUM: 769MG

*C*abbage is a mainstay in northern Europe, where the round, compact vegetable we know today was developed during the Middle Ages. In Russia, cabbage is the basis for soups like this one, made with tomatoes and topped with sour cream. Our interpretation is rounded out with big chunks of beef, carrots, and parsnip.

RUSSIAN CABBAGE AND BEEF SOUP

SERVES: 4
WORKING TIME: 15 MINUTES
TOTAL TIME: 6 TO 8 HOURS

Two 14½-ounce cans no-salt-added stewed tomatoes

1 cup reduced-sodium chicken broth, defatted

2 tablespoons fresh lemon juice

2 teaspoons sugar

1 teaspoon salt

3 cloves garlic, minced

1 pound cabbage, shredded

1 pound well-trimmed top round of beef, cut into ½-inch chunks

1 onion, diced

2 carrots, halved lengthwise and thinly sliced

1 parsnip, peeled, halved lengthwise, and thinly sliced

1 cup snipped fresh dill (see tip)

2 tablespoons reduced-fat sour cream

1. In a 4-quart electric slow cooker, combine the stewed tomatoes, broth, lemon juice, sugar, salt, garlic, and 2 cups of water, stirring until well combined. Add the cabbage, beef, onion, carrots, parsnip, and ¾ cup of the dill. Cover, and with the setting on low, cook for 6 to 8 hours, or until the cabbage and beef are tender.

2. Divide the soup among 4 bowls. Top each with some of the sour cream, sprinkle with the remaining ¼ cup dill, and serve.

Helpful hint: If parsnips are not available, you can substitute another carrot.

FAT: 6G/17%
CALORIES: 321
SATURATED FAT: 1.9G
CARBOHYDRATE: 39G
PROTEIN: 33G
CHOLESTEROL: 67MG
SODIUM: 855MG

TIP

Kitchen shears are the best tool for mincing fresh dill. Hold the dill over a measuring cup and snip off the leaves until you have the amount you need.

CHILI CON CARNE

SERVES: 4
WORKING TIME: 25 MINUTES
TOTAL TIME: 35 MINUTES

½ pound well-trimmed top round of beef, cut into large chunks

2 teaspoons olive oil

5 cloves garlic, minced

6 scallions, thinly sliced

1 large green bell pepper, coarsely chopped

1 jalapeño pepper, minced

1 tablespoon chili powder

½ teaspoon dried thyme

½ teaspoon dried oregano

½ teaspoon ground cumin

½ teaspoon salt

1 tablespoon flour

8-ounce can no-salt-added tomato sauce

½ cup reduced-sodium beef broth

19-ounce can red kidney beans, rinsed and drained

1 cup frozen corn kernels

¼ cup reduced-fat sour cream

1. In a food processor, process the meat until coarsely ground, about 30 seconds.

2. In a large skillet, heat the oil until hot but not smoking over medium heat. Add the garlic and all but 1 tablespoon of the scallions and cook, stirring frequently, until the scallions are softened, about 2 minutes. Add the bell pepper and jalapeño pepper and cook, stirring frequently, until the bell pepper is crisp-tender, about 3 minutes. Stir the meat into the skillet, breaking it up with a spoon. Sprinkle the meat with the chili powder, thyme, oregano, cumin, and salt and cook until the meat is no longer pink, about 2 minutes.

3. Sprinkle the meat evenly with the flour, stirring to combine. Add the tomato sauce, broth, beans, and corn and bring to a boil. Reduce to a simmer, cover, and cook until the flavors are blended and the sauce is slightly thickened, about 7 minutes. Serve with the sour cream sprinkled with the remaining 1 tablespoon scallions.

Helpful hint: You can adjust the heat of the chili by removing the seeds and membranes from the jalapeño. Most of the "burn" resides in this part of chilies, so scraping out and discarding the seeds and ribs makes for a milder dish.

FAT: 8G/24%
CALORIES: 307
SATURATED FAT: 2G
CARBOHYDRATE: 37G
PROTEIN: 25G
CHOLESTEROL: 37MG
SODIUM: 594MG

These days, chili comes in many guises—with beef or pork, chopped or ground, hot or mild, with or without beans—so there are many decisions to be made when cooking up a pot. Here's an easy way out—a recipe for a hearty chili that should please just about everybody. Warm jalapeño corn bread would be a wonderful accompaniment.

BEEF STEW WITH PEANUT SAUCE

SERVES: 4
WORKING TIME: 30 MINUTES
TOTAL TIME: 45 MINUTES

Peanuts—like beans and peas—are legumes, so they're right at home in a robust stew. Serve the stew with rice for a truly hearty dinner.

2 tablespoons flour

½ teaspoon salt

¼ teaspoon cayenne pepper

¾ pound well-trimmed top round of beef, cut into ½-inch cubes

2 teaspoons olive oil

1 red bell pepper, cut into ½-inch-wide strips

1 green bell pepper, cut into ½-inch-wide strips

3 cloves garlic, minced

1 sweet potato (10 ounces), peeled and cut into ½-inch cubes

⅔ cup reduced-sodium beef broth

2 tablespoons creamy peanut butter

1 tablespoon honey

¾ teaspoon ground coriander

¼ teaspoon dried marjoram

1. On a sheet of waxed paper, combine the flour, ¼ teaspoon of the salt, and the cayenne. Dredge the beef in the flour mixture, shaking off the excess.

2. In a nonstick Dutch oven or flameproof casserole, heat the oil until hot but not smoking over medium heat. Add the beef and cook until lightly browned, about 4 minutes. With a slotted spoon, transfer the beef to a plate. Set aside.

3. Add the bell peppers and garlic to the pan and cook until the peppers are crisp-tender, about 4 minutes. Stir in the sweet potato and cook until lightly browned, about 4 minutes.

4. Meanwhile, in a small bowl, combine the broth, peanut butter, honey, coriander, marjoram, and the remaining ¼ teaspoon salt. Stir into the pan and bring to a boil. Reduce to a simmer, cover, and cook until the sweet potato is tender, about 10 minutes. Return the beef to the pan and simmer just until cooked through, about 2 minutes. Divide the stew among 4 plates and serve.

Helpful hint: This stew is an excellent candidate for advance preparation. You can make the stew up to 2 days ahead of time and reheat it over low heat, adding a little water if necessary.

FAT: 9G/29%
CALORIES: 277
SATURATED FAT: 2G
CARBOHYDRATE: 24G
PROTEIN: 24G
CHOLESTEROL: 49MG
SODIUM: 467

SPICY BEER-BRAISED BEEF STEW

SERVES: 4
WORKING TIME: 30 MINUTES
TOTAL TIME: 50 MINUTES

3 tablespoons flour

½ teaspoon salt

¼ teaspoon freshly ground black pepper

1 pound well-trimmed top round of beef, cut into ¾-inch cubes

2 teaspoons olive oil

2 Spanish onions (1 pound), halved and thinly sliced

4 cloves garlic, minced

2 carrots, thinly sliced

1½ cups dark beer

1 cup reduced-sodium chicken broth, defatted

2 tablespoons no-salt-added tomato paste

¾ teaspoon dried thyme

½ teaspoon red pepper flakes

¼ teaspoon ground allspice

¼ cup chopped fresh parsley

1. On a sheet of waxed paper, combine the flour, ¼ teaspoon of the salt, and the pepper. Dredge the beef in the flour mixture, shaking off and reserving the excess. In a nonstick Dutch oven, heat the oil until hot but not smoking over medium heat. Add the beef and cook until lightly browned, about 4 minutes. With a slotted spoon, transfer the beef to a plate. Set aside.

2. Add the onions and garlic to the pan and cook, stirring, until golden brown, about 10 minutes. Add the carrots and cook, stirring frequently, until almost tender, about 5 minutes. Stir in the beer, increase the heat to high, and cook until the beer is reduced by half, about 5 minutes. Stir in the broth, tomato paste, thyme, red pepper flakes, allspice, and the remaining ¼ teaspoon salt. Bring to a boil, reduce to a simmer, cover, and cook until the vegetables are tender, about 10 minutes.

3. In a small bowl, combine the reserved dredging mixture and ¼ cup of water. Stir the flour mixture into the pan and bring to a boil. Cook, stirring, until the sauce is slightly thickened, about 2 minutes. Return the beef to the pan and cook until just cooked through, about 2 minutes. Divide among 4 bowls, sprinkle the parsley over, and serve.

Helpful hint: Sweet Vidalia, Maui, or Granex onions may be substituted for the mild Spanish onions.

FAT: 6G/18%
CALORIES: 302
SATURATED FAT: 1.6G
CARBOHYDRATE: 25G
PROTEIN: 30G
CHOLESTEROL: 65MG
SODIUM: 530MG

Here's our light take on Flemish "carbonnade." Dark beer gives it rich color and a slightly fruity bouquet.

This
is more a vegetable
soup than anything
else, but one that's
liberally laced with
cubes of lean
Canadian bacon. The
bacon infuses the
vegetables, beans,
macaroni, and creamy
broth with a tempting
smoky flavor. Hot
homemade biscuits
would make an ideal
accompaniment for the
savory chowder.

VEGETABLE CHOWDER WITH CANNELLINI AND BACON

SERVES: 4
WORKING TIME: 25 MINUTES
TOTAL TIME: 35 MINUTES

2 teaspoons olive oil

¾ cup diced Canadian bacon (4 ounces)

3 carrots, thinly sliced

2 ribs celery, thinly sliced

3 cloves garlic, minced

¾ pound Savoy or green cabbage, cut into 1-inch pieces (see tip)

¾ teaspoon ground ginger

½ teaspoon freshly ground black pepper

1½ cups reduced-sodium chicken broth, defatted

1½ cups evaporated skimmed milk

4 ounces elbow macaroni

16-ounce can white kidney beans (cannellini), rinsed and drained

⅓ cup snipped fresh dill

¾ teaspoon cornstarch

1. In a Dutch oven or flameproof casserole, heat the oil until hot but not smoking over medium heat. Add the Canadian bacon and cook, stirring frequently, until lightly crisped, about 2 minutes. Add the carrots, celery, and garlic and cook, stirring frequently, until the carrots are crisp-tender, about 4 minutes. Stir in the cabbage, cover, and cook, stirring occasionally, until the cabbage is wilted, about 4 minutes.

2. Add the ginger, pepper, broth, 3 cups of water, and 1 cup of the evaporated milk and bring to a boil. Stir in the macaroni, beans, and all but 2 tablespoons of the dill. Partially cover, and cook, stirring occasionally, until the macaroni is tender, about 8 minutes.

3. Meanwhile, in a small bowl, combine the remaining ½ cup evaporated milk and the cornstarch. Bring the chowder to a boil and stir in the cornstarch mixture. Boil until slightly thickened and creamy, about 1 minute. Sprinkle with the remaining 2 tablespoons dill before serving.

Helpful hint: Savoy cabbage has crinkly yellow-green leaves that form a looser head then regular green cabbage. It is milder in flavor and supplies more of the beneficial nutrient beta carotene than other cabbages.

FAT: 6G/14%
CALORIES: 390
SATURATED FAT: 1.1G
CARBOHYDRATE: 59G
PROTEIN: 27G
CHOLESTEROL: 18MG
SODIUM: 957MG

TIP

To cut the cabbage for this recipe, first halve the head and cut out the dense white core. Cut the cabbage half into 1-inch-wide wedges, then cut the wedges crosswise into 1-inch pieces

Sicilian-Style Ragout of Beef

SERVES: 4
WORKING TIME: 20 MINUTES
TOTAL TIME: 30 MINUTES

Sicilian cuisine upholds an ancient tradition of accenting savory dishes with sweet ingredients: Raisins, oranges, honey, and sweet Marsala wine go into many Sicilian meat, fish, or poultry dishes. This delicious beef ragout, served over golden ribbons of fettuccine, is simmered in a broth flavored with orange juice, raisins, ginger, and fennel seeds.

¼ cup golden raisins
½ cup hot water
2 tablespoons flour
½ teaspoon salt
¼ teaspoon freshly ground black pepper
¾ pound well-trimmed top round of beef, cut into ½-inch cubes
1 tablespoon olive oil
1 large onion, coarsely chopped
4 cloves garlic, minced
6 ounces fettuccine
2 large tomatoes, coarsely chopped
⅓ cup orange juice
½ cup reduced-sodium chicken broth, defatted
½ teaspoon fennel seeds
¼ teaspoon ground ginger

1. Start heating a large pot of water to boiling for the pasta. In a small bowl, combine the raisins and hot water and set aside to soften. On a sheet of waxed paper, combine the flour, ¼ teaspoon of the salt, and the pepper. Dredge the beef in the flour mixture, shaking off the excess.

2. In a Dutch oven or flameproof casserole, heat 2 teaspoons of the oil until hot but not smoking over medium heat. Add the beef and cook until lightly browned, about 4 minutes. With a slotted spoon, transfer the beef to a plate and set aside. Add the remaining 1 teaspoon oil to the pan along with the onion and garlic and cook, stirring frequently, until the onion is lightly golden, about 5 minutes.

3. Cook the fettuccine in the boiling water until just tender. Drain well.

4. Meanwhile, stir the tomatoes, orange juice, and the raisins and their soaking liquid into the stew and bring to a boil. Stir in the broth, fennel seeds, ginger, and the remaining ¼ teaspoon salt and return to a boil. Reduce to a simmer, cover, and cook until the flavors are blended, about 7 minutes. Uncover, return the beef to the pan, and cook until the beef is just cooked through, about 2 minutes. Divide the fettuccine among 4 plates, spoon the beef mixture alongside, and serve.

FAT: 8G/18%
CALORIES: 396
SATURATED FAT: 1.8G
CARBOHYDRATE: 52G
PROTEIN: 28G
CHOLESTEROL: 89MG
SODIUM: 418MG

PORK AND BLACK BEAN STEW

SERVES: 4
WORKING TIME: 25 MINUTES
TOTAL TIME: 40 MINUTES

2 tablespoons flour

½ teaspoon salt

¼ teaspoon freshly ground black pepper

¾ pound well-trimmed pork tenderloin, cut into ½-inch cubes

2 teaspoons olive oil

1 red bell pepper, cut into ½-inch squares

6 scallions, cut into 1-inch pieces

3 cloves garlic, crushed and peeled

1 teaspoon chili powder

¾ teaspoon ground coriander

½ teaspoon ground cumin

¼ cup yellow cornmeal

1 cup reduced-sodium chicken broth, defatted

16-ounce can black beans, rinsed and drained

1 tablespoon honey

1 cup frozen corn kernels

1. On a sheet of waxed paper, combine the flour, ¼ teaspoon of the salt, and the black pepper. Dredge the pork in the flour mixture, shaking off the excess.

2. In a Dutch oven or flameproof casserole, heat the oil until hot but not smoking over medium heat. Add the pork and cook until golden brown, about 4 minutes. With a slotted spoon, transfer the pork to a plate and set aside. Add the bell pepper and cook until tender, about 5 minutes.

3. Meanwhile, in a food processor, combine the scallions, garlic, chili powder, coriander, cumin, cornmeal, and ½ cup of the broth. Process until well combined. Stir the cornmeal mixture into the pan and cook, stirring constantly, until the mixture is slightly thickened, about 4 minutes. Stir in the remaining ½ cup broth, the beans, honey, and remaining ¼ teaspoon salt. Bring to a boil and cook for 5 minutes to blend the flavors.

4. Return the pork to the pan, stir in the corn, and simmer until the pork is cooked through, about 4 minutes.

Helpful hint: Pork tenderloin is the leanest, most tender cut of pork; just 26 percent of its calories come from fat. Pork ribs, by comparison, derive about 56 percent of their calories from fat.

FAT: 6G/18%
CALORIES: 308
SATURATED FAT: 1.4G
CARBOHYDRATE: 38G
PROTEIN: 26G
CHOLESTEROL: 55MG
SODIUM: 673MG

The use of two kinds of corn suggests the Latin American influence in this recipe. Crisp corn kernels dot the stew, while cornmeal thickens the broth. If you add dry cornmeal to hot liquid, it tends to form lumps. With our fail-safe method, you blend the cornmeal with the cool liquid to form what is called a "slurry," then add this mixture to the hot pan.

SAUERBRATEN

SERVES: 4
WORKING TIME: 15 MINUTES
TOTAL TIME: 6 TO 8 HOURS

Cookies in the stew? Can that be right? Yes, gingersnaps are the traditional thickening for this beloved German specialty. Traditionalists marinate the beef for several days, but lengthy simmering (our sauerbraten is made in a slow cooker) serves the same purpose. Accompany the meltingly tender beef and vegetables with thick-sliced dark pumpernickel.

½ cup red wine vinegar

1 tablespoon honey

4 whole cloves

1 bay leaf

½ teaspoon salt

¼ teaspoon freshly ground black pepper

1¼ pounds well-trimmed bottom round of beef, in one piece

1 pound sweet potatoes, peeled and cut into ½-inch chunks

2 cups peeled baby carrots

1 cup frozen pearl onions

¼ cup golden raisins

10 gingersnap cookies (2½ ounces), crumbled

1. In a 4-quart electric slow cooker, combine the vinegar, honey, cloves, bay leaf, salt, pepper, and ¾ cup of water. Add the meat, tossing to coat. Stir in the sweet potatoes, carrots, onions, and raisins. Cover, and with the setting on low, cook until the meat is tender, 6 to 8 hours.

2. Transfer the meat and vegetables to a plate. Stir the gingersnaps into the slow cooker, cover, and cook until the sauce is thickened, 5 to 10 minutes. Thinly slice the meat and divide among 4 plates. Spoon the sauce and vegetables over and serve.

Helpful hint: Bottom round is not only the traditional cut for sauerbraten, it's also among the very leanest cuts of beef. Remember that beef graded Select has considerably less fat than Choice or Prime grades.

FAT: 10G/20%
CALORIES: 453
SATURATED FAT: 3.1G
CARBOHYDRATE: 56G
PROTEIN: 35G
CHOLESTEROL: 84MG
SODIUM: 509MG

ASIAN HOT POT

SERVES: 4
WORKING TIME: 20 MINUTES
TOTAL TIME: 40 MINUTES

With its fragrant broth, thinly sliced beef, slender noodles, and crisp vegetables, this soup resembles Vietnamese "pho bo."

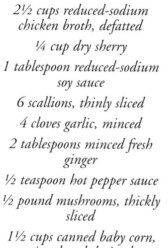

2½ cups reduced-sodium chicken broth, defatted

¼ cup dry sherry

1 tablespoon reduced-sodium soy sauce

6 scallions, thinly sliced

4 cloves garlic, minced

2 tablespoons minced fresh ginger

½ teaspoon hot pepper sauce

½ pound mushrooms, thickly sliced

1½ cups canned baby corn, rinsed and drained

4 ounces vermicelli, broken into short pieces

½ pound well-trimmed top round of beef, cut into thin bite-size pieces

1 bunch watercress, thick stems trimmed

1½ cups bean sprouts

1 cup slivered snow peas

1 tablespoon rice vinegar

2 teaspoons dark Oriental sesame oil

1. In a Dutch oven or large saucepan, combine the broth, 3½ cups of water, the sherry, soy sauce, scallions, garlic, ginger, and hot pepper sauce. Bring to a boil over medium heat, reduce to a simmer, cover, and cook for 10 minutes to blend the flavors.

2. Partially cover the pan and return to a boil. Add the mushrooms, corn, and vermicelli and cook for 6 minutes. Stir in the beef, watercress, bean sprouts, snow peas, vinegar, and sesame oil and cook until the vermicelli is just tender and the beef is medium-rare, about 2 minutes. Divide the beef mixture among 4 bowls and serve.

Helpful hints: You can substitute an equal amount of dry white wine for the sherry. Frozen snow peas may be used if fresh are unavailable.

FAT: 6G/18%
CALORIES: 305
SATURATED FAT: 1.1G
CARBOHYDRATE: 36G
PROTEIN: 25G
CHOLESTEROL: 32MG
SODIUM: 640MG

VEGETABLES

3

*S*tews
usually require long,
slow cooking to render
meat or poultry
perfectly tender. But
meatless stews can cook
considerably quicker.
Tofu and cannellini
(white kidney beans),
the protein components
of this stew, just need
to be heated through;
the vegetables, in true
Asian style, are briefly
cooked until crisp-
tender.

ASIAN-STYLE VEGETABLE STEW WITH TOFU

SERVES: 4
WORKING TIME: 20 MINUTES
TOTAL TIME: 25 MINUTES

1 cup long-grain rice

¼ teaspoon salt

2 teaspoons vegetable oil

4 scallions, thinly sliced

2 cloves garlic, minced

1 red bell pepper, cut into
½-inch pieces

⅓ cup orange juice

¼ cup chili sauce

2 tablespoons plum jam

2 tablespoons reduced-sodium soy
sauce

¾ teaspoon ground ginger

½ pound snow peas, fresh or
frozen, halved crosswise (see tip)

½ cup canned sliced water
chestnuts, drained

19-ounce can white kidney beans
(cannellini), rinsed and drained

8 ounces firm tofu, cut into
½-inch cubes

1. In a medium saucepan, bring 2¼ cups of water to a boil. Add the rice and salt, reduce to a simmer, cover, and cook until the rice is tender, about 17 minutes.

2. Meanwhile, in a large skillet, heat the oil until hot but not smoking over medium heat. Add the scallions and garlic and cook, stirring frequently, until the scallions are tender, about 2 minutes. Add the bell pepper and cook until crisp-tender, about 2 minutes.

3. In a small bowl, combine the orange juice, chili sauce, plum jam, soy sauce, and ginger. Add the orange juice mixture to the skillet, stirring to combine. Add the snow peas and water chestnuts and bring to a boil. Stir in the white kidney beans and cook just until heated through, about 2 minutes. Add the tofu and cook, stirring gently, until heated through, about 3 minutes. Divide the stew among 4 plates, spoon the rice alongside, and serve.

Helpful hint: For this recipe you'll want to buy firm tofu, which looks like little pillows, rather than soft tofu, which comes in straight-edged blocks; soft tofu would crumble apart in the stew.

FAT: 9G/17%
CALORIES: 470
SATURATED FAT: 1.1G
CARBOHYDRATE: 78G
PROTEIN: 23G
CHOLESTEROL: 0MG
SODIUM: 853MG

TIP

To prepare fresh snow peas for cooking, trim the stem end and pull off the string along the straight side. For the best flavor and texture, cook snow peas just until they are crisp-tender and a vibrant green.

Italian Vegetable-Bean Soup with Pesto

Serves: 4
Working time: 25 minutes
Total time: 40 minutes

Pesto, that flavorful blend of basil, nuts, cheese, and olive oil, is more than just a pasta sauce: Italians often add a dollop of pesto to minestrone and other vegetable soups as a seasoning and final enrichment. Our pesto is made without the traditional pine nuts (or walnuts); it's lower in fat, yet it still gives off that familiar glorious fragrance when it hits the steaming broth.

4 teaspoons olive oil

1 red onion, coarsely chopped

3 carrots, thinly sliced

13¾-ounce can reduced-sodium chicken broth, defatted

1 cup dry white wine

¾ teaspoon dried rosemary

⅛ teaspoon red pepper flakes

½ pound small red potatoes, quartered

1 cup packed fresh basil leaves

¼ cup grated Parmesan cheese

2 cloves garlic, peeled

½ pound Italian green beans, fresh or thawed frozen, cut into 1-inch pieces

½ cup small pasta shapes, such as orzo

1 cup frozen peas

19-ounce can white kidney beans (cannellini), rinsed and drained

¼ teaspoon salt

1. In a nonstick Dutch oven or large saucepan, heat 2 teaspoons of the oil until hot but not smoking over medium heat. Add the onion and carrots and cook until the onion is softened, about 5 minutes. Stir in the broth, 1½ cups of water, the wine, rosemary, red pepper flakes, and potatoes. Bring to a simmer and cook until the potatoes are firm-tender, about 8 minutes.

2. Meanwhile, in a food processor or blender, combine the basil, Parmesan, garlic, remaining 2 teaspoons oil, and 2 tablespoons of water. Process to a smooth purée. Set the pesto aside.

3. Add the green beans and pasta to the soup and cook until the pasta and green beans are just tender, about 8 minutes. Stir in the peas, white kidney beans, and salt and simmer until the peas and white kidney beans are heated through, about 3 minutes. Stir in the pesto. Divide among 4 bowls and serve.

Helpful hint: Regular green beans, either fresh or frozen, can be substituted if Italian green beans are not available.

Fat: 8g/16%
Calories: 444
Saturated Fat: 1.7g
Carbohydrate: 67g
Protein: 20g
Cholesterol: 4mg
Sodium: 741mg

BEAN, TOMATO, AND TORTELLINI CHOWDER

SERVES: 4
WORKING TIME: 20 MINUTES
TOTAL TIME: 45 MINUTES

Filled pasta can turn a simple soup into a hearty meal. Here, cheese-filled tortellini, widely available in fresh or frozen form, go into a savory supper dish. Tomato-vegetable juice is the base for the tasty broth; reduced-fat sour cream adds a smooth richness that's balanced by lively accents of fresh mint and lemon juice. Serve a simple green salad on the side.

2½ cups reduced-sodium tomato-vegetable juice

2 leeks, cut into ½-inch dice, or 4 scallions, cut into ½-inch lengths

2 large carrots, halved lengthwise and thinly sliced

1 turnip (6 ounces), peeled and cut into ½-inch dice

3 cloves garlic, minced

¾ teaspoon ground ginger

½ teaspoon salt

1 pound all-purpose potatoes, peeled and cut into ½-inch dice

¼ cup chopped fresh mint

3 tablespoons fresh lemon juice

¾ pound cheese tortellini

½ pound green beans, cut into 1-inch lengths

3 tablespoons reduced-fat sour cream

1. In a Dutch oven or large saucepan, combine 4½ cups of water, the tomato-vegetable juice, leeks, carrots, turnip, garlic, ginger, and salt and bring to a boil over medium heat. Reduce to a simmer, cover, and cook until the vegetables are crisp-tender and the broth is flavorful, about 12 minutes.

2. Add the potatoes, mint, lemon juice, and tortellini and cook for 5 minutes. Add the green beans and cook until the tortellini are tender and the beans are crisp-tender, about 5 minutes. Remove from the heat, stir in the sour cream, divide among 4 bowls, and serve.

Helpful hints: Frozen tortellini may take 2 to 3 minutes longer to cook than fresh. A leek's many layers trap sand and dirt, and it's tricky to get a whole or split leek really clean. When the recipe calls for sliced leeks, like this one, it's easier to wash the vegetable in a bowl of water after cutting it up.

FAT: 8G/15%
CALORIES: 471
SATURATED FAT: 3.3G
CARBOHYDRATE: 85G
PROTEIN: 17G
CHOLESTEROL: 39MG
SODIUM: 831MG

Corn, Barley, and Lima Bean Stew

SERVES: 4
WORKING TIME: 20 MINUTES
TOTAL TIME: 40 MINUTES

1 tablespoon olive oil

1 onion, chopped

3 cloves garlic, chopped

2 teaspoons sage

1 teaspoon dried thyme

2 tablespoons flour

13¾-ounce can reduced-sodium chicken broth, defatted

½ cup quick-cooking barley

¾ pound red potatoes, cut into ½-inch dice

10-ounce package frozen baby lima beans

1 red bell pepper, cut into ½-inch squares

⅛ teaspoon cayenne pepper

1 cup frozen corn kernels

¼ cup chopped fresh parsley

1 teaspoon salt

1. In a Dutch oven or flameproof casserole, heat the oil until hot but not smoking over medium heat. Add the onion and cook, stirring frequently, until the onion is softened and lightly colored, about 6 minutes. Add the garlic, sage, and thyme and cook until fragrant, about 30 seconds. Sprinkle the mixture with the flour, stirring to thoroughly combine.

2. Stir in the broth, 3 cups of water, and the barley. Bring to a boil, reduce to a simmer, cover, and cook for 10 minutes. Add the potatoes, lima beans, bell pepper, and cayenne. Simmer until the barley is tender, about 10 minutes. Stir in the corn, parsley, and salt and simmer until the corn is heated through, about 3 minutes. Divide among 4 bowls and serve.

Helpful hint: You can substitute fresh dill for the fresh parsley if you like.

Barley soup is often made with lamb, but we combine the grain with corn and lima beans, supplying the protein in this substantial, nicely seasoned meatless stew. Our shortcut secret here is quick-cooking barley, which is pre-steamed: It requires about 40 minutes less cooking time than pearl barley, but it's just as nutritious.

FAT: 5G/13%
CALORIES: 347
SATURATED FAT: 0.5G
CARBOHYDRATE: 66G
PROTEIN: 13G
CHOLESTEROL: 0MG
SODIUM: 866MG

SPICED TOMATO-LENTIL STEW

SERVES: 4
WORKING TIME: 20 MINUTES
TOTAL TIME: 1 HOUR

Pulses—lentils, beans, and peas—are the staff of life in India. This Indian-inspired stew is made with both chick-peas and lentils.

1 tablespoon olive oil
1 large onion, coarsely chopped
3 cloves garlic, minced
2 teaspoons paprika
1 teaspoon ground cumin
1 teaspoon ground coriander
1 teaspoon ground ginger
1 pound small red potatoes, quartered
1½ cups lentils, rinsed and picked over
Two 14½-ounce cans no-salt-added stewed tomatoes, chopped with their juices
½ teaspoon salt
16-ounce can chick-peas, rinsed and drained
10-ounce package frozen chopped spinach, thawed
1 tablespoon fresh lemon juice

1. In a large saucepan, heat the oil until hot but not smoking over medium heat. Add the onion and garlic and cook, stirring frequently, until softened, about 7 minutes. Add the paprika, cumin, coriander, and ginger, stirring to coat.

2. Add the potatoes, lentils, tomatoes with their juice, 3½ cups of water, and the salt. Bring to a boil, reduce to a simmer, cover, and cook until the potatoes and lentils are almost tender, about 20 minutes.

3. Stir in the chick-peas, cover, and cook until the potatoes and lentils are very tender, about 10 minutes. Stir in the spinach and lemon juice and cook just until the spinach is heated through, about 5 minutes.

Helpful hint: If you have a pair of kitchen shears, you can save time chopping the tomatoes: Just open the can, insert the blades of the scissors, and chop the tomatoes while they're still in the can.

FAT: 7G/12%
CALORIES: 545
SATURATED FAT: 0.7G
CARBOHYDRATE: 96G
PROTEIN: 32G
CHOLESTEROL: 0MG
SODIUM: 507MG

HERBED TWO-PEA SOUP

SERVES: 4
WORKING TIME: 20 MINUTES
TOTAL TIME: 50 MINUTES

1½ cups split peas, rinsed and picked over

1 baking potato (8 ounces), peeled and thinly sliced

6 scallions, thinly sliced

2 large carrots, thinly sliced

2 tablespoons minced fresh ginger

3 cloves garlic, crushed and peeled

½ cup chopped fresh mint

1 teaspoon salt

½ teaspoon dried sage

¼ teaspoon freshly ground black pepper

2 cups shredded iceberg lettuce

1½ cups frozen peas

1 cup evaporated low-fat (1%) milk

1. In a Dutch oven or large saucepan, combine the split peas, potato, scallions, carrots, ginger, garlic, mint, salt, sage, and pepper. Add 4 cups of water and bring to a boil over medium heat. Reduce to a simmer, cover, and cook until the split peas and potatoes are tender, about 25 minutes.

2. Stir in the lettuce and frozen peas and return to a boil. Reduce to a simmer, cover, and cook until the lettuce is wilted and the peas are heated through, about 5 minutes.

3. Ladle the soup into a large bowl. Working in batches, transfer the soup to a food processor and process until smooth. Return to the Dutch oven along with the evaporated milk and cook until just heated through.

Helpful hint: A hand blender would work well for this recipe. Instead of pouring the soup into a food processor, use the blender right in the pot of soup, as you would an electric mixer.

FAT: 2G/4%
CALORIES: 420
SATURATED FAT: 0.2G
CARBOHYDRATE: 76G
PROTEIN: 28G
CHOLESTEROL: 6MG
SODIUM: 718MG

Ginger, sage, garlic, and mint distinguish this velvety purée from heavier pea soups flavored with ham or sausage.

SPANISH VEGETABLE STEW

SERVES: 4
WORKING TIME: 20 MINUTES
TOTAL TIME: 45 MINUTES

Half an ounce of dried mushrooms may not sound like much, but you'll be amazed at the depth of flavor this ingredient adds to this meatless dish. You'll find reasonably priced imported dried mushrooms at the supermarket; gourmet shops carry more distinctive (and more expensive) varieties, such as porcini (the French call them "cèpes") and shiitakes.

½ ounce dried mushrooms

½ cup boiling water

1 tablespoon olive oil

2 bell peppers, preferably 1 red and 1 green, cut into ½-inch squares

2 large leeks, thinly sliced

2 zucchini, quartered lengthwise and thinly sliced

13¾-ounce can reduced-sodium chicken broth, defatted

14½-ounce can no-salt-added stewed tomatoes

1¼ teaspoons dried thyme

⅛ teaspoon saffron, or 1 teaspoon turmeric

½ cup long-grain rice

15-ounce can hominy or white kidney beans (cannellini), rinsed and drained

1 cup frozen peas

¼ cup dry sherry

1 tablespoon balsamic vinegar

½ teaspoon salt

1. In a small bowl, combine the dried mushrooms and the boiling water and let stand until softened, about 15 minutes. Scoop the dried mushrooms from their soaking liquid, reserve the liquid, then rinse and coarsely chop the mushrooms. Strain the liquid through a paper towel-lined sieve.

2. Meanwhile, in a nonstick Dutch oven or flameproof casserole, heat the oil until hot but not smoking over medium heat. Add the bell peppers and leeks. Cook, stirring frequently, until softened, about 6 minutes.

3. Add the chopped mushrooms, zucchini, broth, tomatoes, thyme, saffron, rice, and the reserved mushroom soaking liquid. Bring to a simmer, cover, and cook for 15 minutes. Stir in the hominy, peas, sherry, vinegar, and salt. Cook until the rice and vegetables are tender, about 5 minutes.

Helpful hint: The finest and most expensive saffron comes in individual threads, which should be gently crumbled just before using and then measured in a measuring spoon. Use the less expensive powdered saffron as you would any other spice.

FAT: 5G/13%
CALORIES: 347
SATURATED FAT: 0.6G
CARBOHYDRATE: 61G
PROTEIN: 14G
CHOLESTEROL: 0MG
SODIUM: 753MG

The jewel-like "island" of fruit is more than just a pretty garnish for this soup: Its sweet-savory balance contrasts with the soup's spices, and the bits of fruit and onion add texture to the smooth purée. Make the topping with mixed dried fruits (sold in bags), or devise your own combination of dried apricots, prunes, raisins, apples, and even cherries.

CURRIED LENTIL SOUP WITH SAVORY FRUIT

SERVES: 4
WORKING TIME: 15 MINUTES
TOTAL TIME: 55 MINUTES

1 cup mixed dried fruit

1 cup boiling water

4 teaspoons olive oil

2 large onions, diced

3 cloves garlic, minced

1⅓ cups lentils, rinsed and picked over

1 large sweet potato (8 ounces), peeled, halved lengthwise, and thinly sliced

2 carrots, thinly sliced

2 tablespoons no-salt-added tomato paste

2 teaspoons curry powder

1 teaspoon ground ginger

½ teaspoon salt

¼ teaspoon freshly ground black pepper

½ cup carrot juice (see tip)

¼ cup reduced-fat sour cream

1. In a small heatproof bowl, combine the fruit and the boiling water. Set aside until softened, about 10 minutes. Drain and coarsely chop the fruit.

2. Meanwhile, in a Dutch oven or large saucepan, heat 2 teaspoons of the oil until hot but not smoking over medium heat. Add 1 of the onions and the garlic and cook, stirring frequently, until the onion is softened, about 7 minutes. Stir in the lentils, sweet potato, carrots, tomato paste, curry powder, ginger, salt, and pepper. Add 4 cups of water and the carrot juice, bring to a boil, reduce to a simmer, cover, and cook until the lentils, potatoes, and carrots are very tender, about 30 minutes. Ladle the soup into a large bowl. Working in batches, transfer the soup to a food processor and process to a smooth purée. Return to the Dutch oven, add the sour cream, and stir to combine.

3. Meanwhile, in a small skillet, heat the remaining 2 teaspoons oil until hot but not smoking over medium-high heat. Add the remaining onion and cook, stirring frequently, until golden brown, about 7 minutes. Add the drained, softened fruit and cook until heated through, about 2 minutes. Ladle the soup into 4 bowls, top with the fruit mixture, and serve.

FAT: 8G/14%
CALORIES: 502
SATURATED FAT: 1.8G
CARBOHYDRATE: 91G
PROTEIN: 23G
CHOLESTEROL: 5MG
SODIUM: 331MG

TIP

Carrot juice, an excellent source of beta carotene and potassium, is a useful soup ingredient. You'll find it in health-food stores, where it's made fresh, and in the refrigerated section of most supermarkets. You may also be able to find it canned, along with other fruit and vegetable juices, in your supermarket.

Ratatouille Stew with Feta

SERVES: 4
WORKING TIME: 25 MINUTES
TOTAL TIME: 40 MINUTES

1 teaspoon olive oil

1 red onion, coarsely chopped

*1 green bell pepper, cut into
¾-inch squares*

*1 eggplant (1 pound), cut into
¾-inch cubes*

*1 zucchini, cut into ¾-inch
cubes*

4 cloves garlic, thinly sliced

*½ pound small mushrooms,
quartered*

*½ cup reduced-sodium chicken
broth, defatted*

*14½-ounce can no-salt-added
stewed tomatoes*

*2 tablespoons no-salt-added
tomato paste*

1 teaspoon red wine vinegar

1 teaspoon dried tarragon

1 teaspoon dried basil

¾ teaspoon salt

¼ teaspoon black pepper

*¾ cup crumbled feta cheese
(3 ounces)*

*4 ounces French bread, cut into
½-inch slices and toasted*

1. In a nonstick Dutch oven or flameproof casserole, heat the oil until hot but not smoking over medium heat. Add the onion and bell pepper and cook until softened, about 4 minutes. Add the eggplant, zucchini, and garlic. Cover and cook, stirring occasionally, for 10 minutes.

2. Add the mushrooms, broth, tomatoes, tomato paste, vinegar, tarragon, basil, salt, and black pepper. Simmer, covered, until the vegetables are crisp-tender, about 6 minutes. Spoon the stew onto 4 plates, top with the feta cheese, and serve with the toast.

Helpful hint: For a change, you might enjoy the ratatouille topped with Roquefort or some other blue cheese instead of the feta.

FAT: 7G/24%
CALORIES: 259
SATURATED FAT: 3.6G
CARBOHYDRATE: 42G
PROTEIN: 11G
CHOLESTEROL: 19MG
SODIUM: 940MG

One of the best-known dishes of Provence, ratatouille is a colorful mixture of summer vegetables that typically includes tomatoes, bell peppers, eggplant, and zucchini. Although it's usually served as a side dish, we've upgraded ratatouille to a satisfying main course. In the traditional method, the vegetables are braised in plenty of olive oil; we've used broth as a cooking medium instead.

VEGETARIAN CHILI

SERVES: 4
WORKING TIME: 35 MINUTES
TOTAL TIME: 45 MINUTES

½ cup bulghur (cracked wheat)

1 cup boiling water

1 tablespoon olive oil

8 scallions, thinly sliced

3 cloves garlic, minced

2 green bell peppers, cut into ½-inch squares

1 pickled jalapeño pepper, seeded and minced

2 large carrots, thinly sliced

2 teaspoons chili powder

1 teaspoon ground cumin

1 teaspoon dried oregano

½ teaspoon salt

Two 19-ounce cans black beans, rinsed and drained

14½-ounce can no-salt-added stewed tomatoes, chopped with their juices

8-ounce can no-salt-added tomato sauce

¼ cup reduced-fat sour cream

1. In a small bowl, combine the bulghur and the boiling water. Set aside to soak while you prepare the rest of the chili.

2. In a Dutch oven or large saucepan, heat the oil until hot but not smoking over medium heat. Add 6 of the scallions and the garlic and cook until softened, about 2 minutes. Add the bell peppers and jalapeño and cook, stirring frequently, until the bell peppers are crisp-tender, about 4 minutes. Add the carrots and cook, stirring frequently, until they are crisp-tender, about 4 minutes.

3. Add the chili powder, cumin, oregano, and salt, stirring to combine. Add the black beans, stewed tomatoes, and tomato sauce and bring to a boil. Drain the bulghur and add it to the pan. Reduce to a simmer, cover, and cook until the chili is slightly thickened and the flavors are blended, about 7 minutes. Serve with the sour cream and the remaining scallions.

Helpful hint: Bulghur is a pre-steamed form of cracked wheat; either product can be used in this recipe.

This chili boasts a deceptively meaty texture, but don't be fooled—it's made with bulghur, not ground beef. Bulghur only requires steeping in water to soften it. Here, you steep the grain while cooking the vegetables, then add the bulghur to the chili just to heat it through. Serve the chili with white or brown rice or steamed tortillas.

FAT: 8G/20%
CALORIES: 363
SATURATED FAT: 1.6G
CARBOHYDRATE: 62G
PROTEIN: 17G
CHOLESTEROL: 5MG
SODIUM: 841MG

VEGETABLE JAMBALAYA

SERVES: 4
WORKING TIME: 35 MINUTES
TOTAL TIME: 55 MINUTES

F*eel*
free to try other
vegetables in this dish.
Jambalaya varies with
the cook, the season,
and what looks good
in the garden.

1 tablespoon olive oil

1 large onion, coarsely diced

4 cloves garlic, minced

*1 red bell pepper, cut into
1-inch squares*

*1 yellow summer squash,
halved lengthwise and cut into
½-inch-thick slices*

*6 ounces small mushrooms,
halved*

1 tomato, coarsely chopped

*1 cup frozen black-eyed peas,
thawed*

1½ teaspoons ground cumin

1 teaspoon dried thyme

¾ teaspoon salt

*¼ teaspoon freshly ground
black pepper*

¼ teaspoon hot pepper sauce

*10-ounce package frozen cut
okra*

*16-ounce can red kidney beans,
rinsed and drained*

1. In a Dutch oven or large saucepan, heat the oil until hot but not smoking over medium heat. Add the onion and garlic and cook, stirring frequently, until the onion is softened, about 7 minutes. Add the bell pepper, squash, and mushrooms and cook, stirring frequently, until the bell pepper is crisp-tender, about 5 minutes.

2. Add the tomato and cook for 2 minutes. Stir in the black-eyed peas, cumin, thyme, salt, black pepper, hot pepper sauce, and 1 cup of water. Bring to a boil, reduce to a simmer, cover, and cook for 10 minutes. Add the okra and beans and return to a boil. Reduce to a simmer, cover, and cook until the vegetables are tender and the beans are warmed through, about 10 minutes. Divide the vegetable mixture among 4 bowls and serve.

Helpful hint: Okra ia a traditional jambalaya ingredient: As it cooks, it releases a substance that thickens the broth. If you like, you can use fresh okra instead of the frozen. Buy small pods about 3 inches long, wash them thoroughly, thinly slice them, and add them to the pan along with the black-eyed peas in step 2.

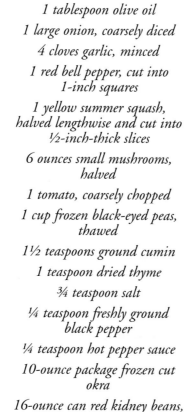

FAT: 5G/19%
CALORIES: 243
SATURATED FAT: 0.7G
CARBOHYDRATE: 40G
PROTEIN: 13G
CHOLESTEROL: 0MG
SODIUM: 575MG

Spicy Three-Squash Stew

SERVES: 4
WORKING TIME: 15 MINUTES
TOTAL TIME: 35 MINUTES

13¾-ounce can reduced-sodium chicken broth, defatted

½ cup long-grain rice

3 cloves garlic, minced

¾ pound butternut squash, peeled and cut into ¾-inch cubes

2 tablespoons red wine vinegar

2 tablespoons molasses

1½ teaspoons ground ginger

½ teaspoon ground allspice

1 zucchini, quartered lengthwise and thinly sliced

1 yellow summer squash, quartered lengthwise and thinly sliced

4 scallions, thinly sliced

2 bananas, coarsely chopped

19-ounce can black beans or pinto beans, rinsed and drained

½ teaspoon salt

⅛ teaspoon cayenne pepper

1. In a Dutch oven or large saucepan, bring the broth and 2 cups of water to a boil over high heat. Add the rice and garlic, reduce the heat to a simmer, cover, and cook for 8 minutes. Add the butternut squash, vinegar, molasses, ginger, and allspice. Cover and cook for 5 minutes to blend the flavors.

2. Add the zucchini and yellow squash and simmer until the butternut squash is firm-tender and the rice is tender, about 5 minutes. Add the scallions, bananas, beans, salt, and cayenne. Cook until warmed through, about 3 minutes. Divide among 4 bowls and serve.

Helpful hint: Molasses comes in a number of grades, reflecting how long it has been boiled; boiling thickens the syrup and reduces its sweetness. Light molasses is mild and sweet, good for many cooking purposes such as this one; dark molasses, thicker and less sweet, is often used in baking; and blackstrap molasses, the darkest and thickest, has a strong, pungent flavor.

FAT: 1G/3%
CALORIES: 304
SATURATED FAT: 0.2G
CARBOHYDRATE: 66G
PROTEIN: 11G
CHOLESTEROL: 0MG
SODIUM: 772MG

Starchy vegetables, rice, and beans add up to a wholesome, satisfying stew. Chopped bananas add a mild sweetness.

Dense,
firm root vegetables
and beans become
tender and richly
flavorful in this easy
one-pot meal, thanks
to slow cooking and
warm seasonings—
ginger, garlic, and
paprika. Knowing that
a steaming stew awaits
you at home is enough
to make the busiest
day go more smoothly.
All you have to do at
dinnertime is open the
pot, stir in the salt
and parsley, and serve.

100

Winter Bean Stew with Barley

Serves: 4
Working time: 15 minutes
Total time: 7 to 9 hours

1 cup dried baby lima beans, rinsed and picked over

⅔ cup dried navy beans, rinsed and picked over

1 pound all-purpose potatoes, peeled and cut into 1-inch chunks

2 carrots, halved lengthwise and cut into 1-inch lengths

1 large onion, coarsely diced

1 parsnip, peeled, halved lengthwise, and cut into 1-inch lengths

½ pound rutabaga, peeled and cut into 1-inch chunks (see tip)

6 cloves garlic, slivered

2 tablespoons pearl barley

1 tablespoon olive oil

2½ teaspoons paprika

1 teaspoon ground ginger

¼ teaspoon freshly ground black pepper

1 teaspoon salt

¼ cup chopped fresh parsley

1. In a medium pot, combine the dried beans with enough water to cover them by 2 inches. Bring to a boil, boil for 2 minutes, cover, and let stand for 1 hour. Drain well.

2. In a 4-quart electric slow cooker, combine the soaked beans, potatoes, carrots, onion, parsnip, rutabaga, garlic, barley, oil, paprika, ginger, pepper, and 4 cups of water. Cover, and with the setting on low, cook until the beans and vegetables are tender, 6 to 8 hours. Stir in the salt and parsley and serve.

Helpful hint: To save time in the morning, start the beans the night before: Put them in a bowl with water to cover by 2 inches and place in the refrigerator to soak overnight. The next morning, drain the beans and assemble the stew in the slow cooker.

FAT: 5G/9%
CALORIES: 506
SATURATED FAT: 0.8G
CARBOHYDRATE: 95G
PROTEIN: 24G
CHOLESTEROL: 0MG
SODIUM: 597MG

TIP

The skin of a rutabaga is quite thick and is often coated with a heavy layer of wax; pare it with a knife rather than a vegetable peeler. After paring, cut the rutabaga into 1-inch-thick slices, then cut the slices into cubes.

VEGETABLE COUSCOUS SOUP

SERVES: 4
WORKING TIME: 35 MINUTES
TOTAL TIME: 50 MINUTES

Couscous, the beadlike North African pasta, is quite different from the elbow macaroni or egg noodles we customarily use in soup. The couscous functions almost like barley or rice in this recipe, adding substance to an unusual combination of vegetables. The soup's spices—cumin, coriander, paprika, and ginger—are flavorings traditionally used with couscous.

4 teaspoons olive oil

1¼ teaspoons ground cumin

1¼ teaspoons ground coriander

1¼ teaspoons paprika

1 teaspoon ground ginger

1 teaspoon salt

½ teaspoon freshly ground black pepper

2 leeks, halved lengthwise and cut into ½-inch-thick slices, or 4 scallions, cut into ½-inch lengths

2 large carrots, thinly sliced

2 large parsnips, peeled and thinly sliced

1 red bell pepper, cut into ½-inch squares

¾ pound butternut squash, peeled and cut into ½-inch chunks

½ cup couscous

1. In a large saucepan, heat the oil until hot but not smoking over medium heat. Add the cumin, coriander, paprika, ginger, salt, and black pepper and cook until fragrant, about 30 seconds.

2. Stir in the leeks, reduce the heat to low, cover, and cook, stirring frequently, until the leeks are softened, about 5 minutes. Add the carrots, parsnips, and bell pepper, stirring to coat. Add ½ cup of water, cover, and cook, stirring frequently, until the carrots are tender, about 7 minutes.

3. Add 4 cups of water and bring to a boil. Add the butternut squash, reduce to a simmer, cover, and cook until the squash is tender and the broth is flavorful, about 10 minutes. Stir in the couscous and boil for 2 minutes. Remove the pan from the heat, cover, and let stand until the couscous is tender, about 3 minutes. Ladle the soup into 4 bowls and serve.

Helpful hint: A leek's many layers trap sand and dirt, and it's tricky to get a whole or split leek really clean. When the recipe calls for sliced leeks, like this one, it's easier to wash the vegetable in a bowl of water after cutting it up.

FAT: 6G/19%
CALORIES: 280
SATURATED FAT: 0.7G
CARBOHYDRATE: 54G
PROTEIN: 6G
CHOLESTEROL: 0MG
SODIUM: 593MG

SQUASH AND CORN CHOWDER

SERVES: 4
WORKING TIME: 25 MINUTES
TOTAL TIME: 45 MINUTES

1 tablespoon olive oil

1 large onion, diced

3 cloves garlic, minced

1 green bell pepper, cut into ¼-inch dice

1 baking potato (8 ounces), peeled and cut into ¼-inch dice

1 carrot, halved lengthwise and thinly sliced

1 zucchini, quartered lengthwise and cut into ½-inch-thick slices

1¼ teaspoons dried tarragon

¾ teaspoon salt

¼ teaspoon cayenne pepper

10-ounce package frozen winter squash purée, thawed

10-ounce package frozen corn kernels, thawed

1 cup evaporated low-fat (1%) milk

1½ teaspoons cornstarch mixed with 1 tablespoon water

1. In a nonstick Dutch oven or large saucepan, heat the oil until hot but not smoking over medium heat. Add the onion and garlic and cook, stirring occasionally, until the onion is softened, about 7 minutes. Add the bell pepper and cook, stirring occasionally, until the pepper is crisp-tender, about 2 minutes.

2. Add the potato, carrot, zucchini, tarragon, salt, and cayenne, stirring to coat. Add 3 cups of water, bring to a boil, reduce to a simmer, cover, and cook until the vegetables are tender, about 10 minutes.

3. Stir in the squash purée, corn, and evaporated milk and simmer, uncovered, until the soup is richly flavored, about 5 minutes. Return to a boil, add the cornstarch mixture, and cook, stirring constantly, until slightly thickened, about 1 minute.

Helpful hints: Combining cornstarch with water before adding it to the chowder helps keep the cornstarch from lumping. To further ensure a lump-free soup, stir or whisk the chowder constantly as you add the cornstarch mixture. If you can't find evaporated low-fat milk, you can substitute the same amount of evaporated skimmed milk.

FAT: 5G/17%
CALORIES: 267
SATURATED FAT: 0.6G
CARBOHYDRATE: 50G
PROTEIN: 11G
CHOLESTEROL: 6MG
SODIUM: 498MG

Y*ou can clearly see the zucchini in this chowder, but there's a second kind of squash in the pot as well: Puréed winter squash (readily available in frozen form), plays an important supporting role as the source of the chowder's cheerful golden color and lush texture. Evaporated milk (the low-fat type) and cornstarch also contribute to the velvety quality of this healthful dish.*

Bean soups are found all over the world, from the Caribbean's spicy black-bean version to Tuscany's sage-infused white-bean purée to meaty, stewlike French garbure. Our slow cooker rendition is Cuban-style; the mixture of oranges and bell peppers that tops the soup is an elaboration on the lemon slices that often garnish black bean soup.

Black Bean Soup with Orange-Pepper Topping

SERVES: 4
WORKING TIME: 20 MINUTES
TOTAL TIME: 7 TO 9 HOURS

2 cups dried black beans, rinsed and picked over

2 red bell peppers, cut into ½-inch squares

1 green bell pepper, cut into ½-inch squares

1 onion, coarsely chopped

6 cloves garlic, slivered

14½-ounce can no-salt-added stewed tomatoes

3 tablespoons no-salt-added tomato paste

2 tablespoons red wine vinegar

2 teaspoons dried oregano

2 teaspoons dried tarragon

1¼ teaspoons salt

2 navel oranges, peeled, sectioned (see tip), and cut into ½-inch pieces

2 tablespoons fresh lime juice

1 tablespoon honey

¼ teaspoon hot pepper sauce

1. In a medium pot, combine the dried beans with enough water to cover them by 2 inches. Bring to a boil, boil for 2 minutes, cover, and let stand for 1 hour. Drain well.

2. In a 4-quart electric slow cooker, combine the drained beans, half of the red bell peppers, the green bell pepper, onion, garlic, tomatoes, tomato paste, vinegar, oregano, tarragon, and 3½ cups of water. Cover, and with the setting on low, cook until the beans are tender, 6 to 8 hours. Stir in 1 teaspoon of the salt.

3. In a medium bowl, combine the orange pieces, lime juice, honey, the remaining ¼ teaspoon salt, the hot pepper sauce, and the remaining red bell pepper. Working in batches if necessary, transfer the soup to a food processor and process to a smooth purée. Divide the soup among 4 bowls, top with the orange-pepper mixture, and serve.

Helpful hints: A hand blender would work well for this recipe. Instead of pouring the soup into a food processor, use the blender right in the pot of soup, as you would an electric mixer. To save time in the morning, presoak the beans overnight: Place them in a bowl with water to cover by 2 inches, cover, and refrigerate. The next morning, drain the beans and assemble the stew in the slow cooker.

TIP

To section the oranges, remove the peel and, using a small knife, trim away all the bitter white pith. Working over a sieve set over a bowl to catch the juices, cut between the membranes to release the orange sections.

FAT: 2G/4%
CALORIES: 467
SATURATED FAT: 0.4G
CARBOHYDRATE: 94G
PROTEIN: 25G
CHOLESTEROL: 0MG
SODIUM: 729MG

PICADILLO-STYLE LENTIL STEW

SERVES: 4
WORKING TIME: 15 MINUTES
TOTAL TIME: 50 MINUTES

Picadillo is the Spanish word for hash. We've used chili powder and raisins—typical ingredients of a Mexican picadillo—in our lentil version.

2 teaspoons olive oil

1 Spanish onion, coarsely chopped

1 cup lentils, rinsed and picked over

4 cloves garlic, minced

Two 8-ounce cans no-salt-added tomato sauce

1 large zucchini (10 ounces), cut into ½-inch dice

1 green bell pepper, cut into ¾-inch squares

¼ cup pimiento-stuffed green olives, finely chopped

¼ cup golden raisins

1 tablespoon chili powder

2 teaspoons ground cumin

1 teaspoon unsweetened cocoa powder

1 teaspoon sugar

1 teaspoon salt

½ teaspoon hot pepper sauce

1. In a large nonstick saucepan, heat the oil until hot but not smoking over medium heat. Add the onion and cook until softened, about 5 minutes. Add the lentils, garlic, and 2½ cups of water. Bring to a simmer, cover, and cook, stirring occasionally, until the lentils are almost tender, about 25 minutes.

2. Stir in the tomato sauce, zucchini, bell pepper, olives, raisins, chili powder, cumin, cocoa powder, sugar, salt, and hot pepper sauce. Bring to a simmer and cook until the squash and bell pepper are tender, about 10 minutes. Divide the stew among 4 bowls and serve.

Helpful hint: You may be wondering why there's cocoa powder in this savory stew: Chocolate is often used in rich Mexican chili sauces to deepen both the flavor and color. You won't taste it in the finished dish.

FAT: 5G/14%
CALORIES: 317
SATURATED FAT: 0.5G
CARBOHYDRATE: 55G
PROTEIN: 18G
CHOLESTEROL: 0MG
SODIUM: 831MG

FISH & SHELLFISH

4

Fish Chowder Primavera

SERVES: 4
WORKING TIME: 25 MINUTES
TOTAL TIME: 45 MINUTES

Fresh, delicate flavors characterize this chowder. Clam juice serves as a convenient substitute for fish stock, but it's diluted with water so as not to overpower the gentle taste of the cod. Zucchini, yellow summer squash, and green peas provide a springlike contrast to the sturdy potatoes; a combination of low-fat milk and cornstarch gives the broth a light creaminess.

1 tablespoon olive oil

1 onion, coarsely chopped

¾ pound all-purpose potatoes, peeled and cut into ½-inch chunks

½ cup bottled clam juice

1 zucchini, halved lengthwise and cut into ½-inch-thick slices

1 yellow summer squash, halved lengthwise and cut into ½-inch-thick slices

¾ teaspoon salt

½ teaspoon dried thyme

½ teaspoon freshly ground black pepper

1½ pounds skinless cod fillets, cut into 1-inch chunks

1 cup frozen peas

¾ cup low-fat (1%) milk

1½ teaspoons cornstarch mixed with 1 tablespoon water

1. In a nonstick Dutch oven or flameproof casserole, heat the oil until hot but not smoking over medium heat. Add the onion and cook, stirring frequently, until golden brown, about 7 minutes. Add the potatoes, stirring to coat. Add the clam juice and 1 cup of water and bring to a boil. Reduce the heat to a simmer, cover, and cook until the potatoes are firm-tender, about 5 minutes.

2. Stir in the zucchini, yellow squash, ½ teaspoon of the salt, ¼ teaspoon of the thyme, and the pepper and cook until the vegetables are tender, about 5 minutes.

3. Place the cod on top of the vegetables and sprinkle with the remaining ¼ teaspoon salt and ¼ teaspoon thyme. Add the peas, pour the milk on top, and bring to a boil. Reduce the heat to a simmer, cover, and cook until the fish is just opaque, about 5 minutes. Return to a boil, add the cornstarch mixture, and cook, stirring constantly, until slightly thickened, about 1 minute.

Helpful hint: Other firm, white-fleshed fish, such as haddock, hake, or pollock, may be substituted for the cod.

FAT: 5G/15%
CALORIES: 308
SATURATED FAT: 1G
CARBOHYDRATE: 28G
PROTEIN: 37G
CHOLESTEROL: 75MG
SODIUM: 639MG

Asian soups sometimes amount to a sort of liquid still-life painting, with each component retaining its own color, shape, texture, and flavor against a background of rich broth. This is true here, where the well-seasoned chicken broth surrounds shrimp, bright squares of bell pepper, diminutive ears of corn, slender noodles, and scallion slices.

SPICY ASIAN-STYLE SHRIMP SOUP

SERVES: 4
WORKING TIME: 30 MINUTES
TOTAL TIME: 40 MINUTES

6 ounces linguine

1 tablespoon olive oil

8 scallions, thinly sliced

5 cloves garlic, minced

1 yellow or red bell pepper, cut into ½-inch squares

2 tomatoes, coarsely chopped

2 cups reduced-sodium chicken broth, defatted

2 tablespoons cider vinegar

2 tablespoons reduced-sodium soy sauce

1 teaspoon sugar

¾ teaspoon ground ginger

½ teaspoon red pepper flakes

1½ pounds shrimp, shelled, deveined (see tip), and halved crosswise

1 cup canned baby corn, rinsed and drained

1. In a large pot of boiling water, cook the linguine until just tender. Drain well.

2. Meanwhile, in a nonstick Dutch oven or flameproof casserole, heat the oil until hot but not smoking over medium heat. Add 6 of the scallions and the garlic and cook until the scallions are softened, about 2 minutes. Add the bell pepper and cook, stirring frequently, until tender, about 4 minutes.

3. Stir in the tomatoes, broth, vinegar, soy sauce, sugar, ginger, red pepper flakes, and 1 cup of water and bring to a boil. Reduce to a simmer, cover, and cook for 5 minutes to blend the flavors. Add the shrimp, corn, and drained pasta and cook until the shrimp are just opaque and the pasta and corn are warmed through, about 3 minutes. Sprinkle with the remaining scallions and serve.

Helpful hint: Canned baby corn, often used in Chinese cooking, is sold in cans or jars in many supermarkets and in Asian grocery stores.

FAT: 7G/16%
CALORIES: 401
SATURATED FAT: 1G
CARBOHYDRATE: 46G
PROTEIN: 38G
CHOLESTEROL: 211MG
SODIUM: 850MG

TIP

To shell fresh shrimp, pull apart the shell at the belly of the shrimp with your fingers, splitting the shell, and remove. To devein, with the point of a sharp knife, score the shrimp along the back, and remove the dark vein.

New Orleans Spicy Shrimp Stew

SERVES: 4
WORKING TIME: 25 MINUTES
TOTAL TIME: 40 MINUTES

1 tablespoon olive oil

1 red bell pepper, cut into ½-inch squares

1 green bell pepper, cut into ½-inch squares

4 scallions, thinly sliced

3 cloves garlic, minced

1 cup reduced-sodium chicken broth, defatted

1 teaspoon dried thyme

½ teaspoon salt

½ teaspoon hot pepper sauce

¼ teaspoon freshly ground black pepper

10-ounce package frozen cut okra

1 pound large shrimp, shelled and deveined

1½ cups frozen corn kernels

1½ teaspoons cornstarch mixed with 1 tablespoon water

1. In a Dutch oven, heat the oil until hot but not smoking over medium heat. Add the bell peppers, scallions, and garlic and cook, stirring frequently, until the peppers are tender, about 5 minutes.

2. Add the broth, thyme, salt, hot pepper sauce, and black pepper and bring to a boil. Add the okra, reduce the heat to a simmer, cover, and cook until the okra is tender, about 7 minutes. Add the shrimp and corn, cover, and cook until the shrimp are just opaque, about 3 minutes. Return to a boil, add the cornstarch mixture, and cook, stirring constantly, until slightly thickened, about 1 minute.

Helpful hints: When you buy a pound of large shrimp, you should get about 16 to 20 shrimp. If you can handle a little more spice, feel free to add an additional ¼ teaspoon hot pepper sauce in step 2.

FAT: 6G/24%
CALORIES: 230
SATURATED FAT: 0.9G
CARBOHYDRATE: 24G
PROTEIN: 23G
CHOLESTEROL: 140MG
SODIUM: 599MG

The food-loving city of New Orleans is surrounded by water; it's set in the Mississippi delta, with Lake Pontchartrain to the north, the Gulf of Mexico to the east, and bayous all around. So it's understandable that shellfish—notably shrimp, oysters, crabs, and crayfish—are favorite foods. This peppery Creole-style stew features lots of tasty shrimp along with okra, corn, and peppers.

Though some New England clam chowder snobs dismiss Manhattan clam chowder as simply "vegetable soup with clams," most serious chowder lovers would agree that each of these two distinctly different soups has its own charms. A green salad with red onions complements our light Manhattan chowder made with white wine and fresh tomatoes.

Manhattan Clam Chowder

SERVES: 4
WORKING TIME: 25 MINUTES
TOTAL TIME: 40 MINUTES

1 cup dry white wine

1 onion, coarsely diced

6 cloves garlic, minced

2 dozen littleneck or other small hard-shell clams, well scrubbed

½ pound all-purpose potatoes, peeled and cut into ¼-inch dice

1 carrot, cut into ¼-inch dice

1 rib celery, cut into ¼-inch dice

2 tomatoes, coarsely chopped

1 bay leaf

½ teaspoon dried thyme

¼ teaspoon salt

¼ cup chopped fresh parsley

1. In a large skillet, combine the wine, onion, and garlic and bring to a boil over medium heat. Add the clams, cover, and cook until the clams have opened, about 5 minutes. Check the clams periodically and remove them as they open; discard any clams that do not open. When cool enough to handle, remove the clams from their shells (see tip) and coarsely chop.

2. Meanwhile, transfer the cooking liquid to a large saucepan and add 2 cups of water. Bring to a boil over medium heat and add the potatoes, carrot, and celery. Reduce to a simmer, cover, and cook until the potatoes are tender, about 5 minutes. Add the tomatoes, bay leaf, thyme, and salt. Cover and cook until the soup is richly flavored, about 5 minutes. Return the chopped clams to the pan and remove the bay leaf. Ladle the soup into 4 bowls, sprinkle with the parsley, and serve.

Helpful hint: Clams sold in the shell should be alive when you buy them. The shells of live clams will be shut tight—or if slightly open, should close immediately when tapped. Store live clams in the refrigerator, covered with damp paper towels. Use them within a day of purchase, and discard any that have opened before cooking.

FAT: 1G/6%
CALORIES: 148
SATURATED FAT: 0.1G
CARBOHYDRATE: 21G
PROTEIN: 14G
CHOLESTEROL: 31MG
SODIUM: 216MG

TIP

To prepare fresh clams, cook them just until the shells open. Unopened clams will be spoiled, so they must be discarded. When cool enough to handle, spread the shells apart and use a fork to pry the clam muscle from the shell.

PROVENÇAL FISH SOUP

SERVES: 4
WORKING TIME: 25 MINUTES
TOTAL TIME: 35 MINUTES

*P*asta, tomatoes, fennel, and swordfish make this citrus-touched soup— bursting with the flavors of Provence— an all-weather delight.

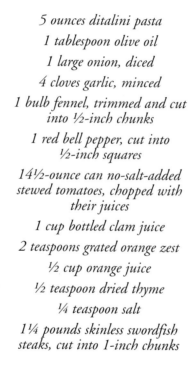

5 ounces ditalini pasta

1 tablespoon olive oil

1 large onion, diced

4 cloves garlic, minced

1 bulb fennel, trimmed and cut into ½-inch chunks

1 red bell pepper, cut into ½-inch squares

14½-ounce can no-salt-added stewed tomatoes, chopped with their juices

1 cup bottled clam juice

2 teaspoons grated orange zest

½ cup orange juice

½ teaspoon dried thyme

¼ teaspoon salt

1¼ pounds skinless swordfish steaks, cut into 1-inch chunks

1. In a medium pot of boiling water, cook the ditalini until just tender. Drain well.

2. In a Dutch oven or flameproof casserole, heat the oil until hot but not smoking over medium heat. Add the onion and garlic and cook, stirring frequently, until the onion is softened, about 7 minutes. Add the fennel and bell pepper, and cook, stirring frequently, until the fennel and bell pepper are crisp-tender, about 5 minutes.

3. Stir in the tomatoes, clam juice, orange zest, orange juice, thyme, salt, and 1 cup of water. Bring to a boil, reduce to a simmer, cover, and cook for 5 minutes to blend the flavors. Add the fish and pasta, cover, and simmer until the fish is just opaque, about 5 minutes. Ladle into 4 soup bowls and serve.

Helpful hint: If you can't find fennel, substitute the same amount of celery chunks and add ¼ teaspoon fennel seeds to the soup.

FAT: 10G/21%
CALORIES: 420
SATURATED FAT: 2.1G
CARBOHYDRATE: 46G
PROTEIN: 36G
CHOLESTEROL: 55MG
SODIUM: 492MG

Greek-Style Cod and Lemon Soup

Serves: 4
Working time: 20 minutes
Total time: 30 minutes

2 cups reduced-sodium chicken broth, defatted

½ teaspoon grated lemon zest

¼ cup fresh lemon juice

½ cup chopped fresh mint

4 scallions, finely chopped

2 cloves garlic, minced

½ teaspoon dried oregano

½ teaspoon salt

½ cup orzo or other small pasta shape

1 yellow summer squash, halved lengthwise and thinly sliced

1½ pounds skinless cod fillets, cut into large pieces

1 teaspoon cornstarch mixed with 1 tablespoon water

1. In a large nonaluminum saucepan, combine 4 cups of water, the broth, lemon zest, lemon juice, mint, scallions, garlic, oregano, and salt. Bring to a boil over medium heat and cook for 5 minutes to blend the flavors.

2. Add the orzo and yellow squash to the pan and cook for 5 minutes. Reduce to a simmer, add the fish, and cook until just opaque, about 4 minutes. Bring to a boil, add the cornstarch mixture, and cook, stirring constantly, until the soup is slightly thickened, about 1 minute. Divide the soup among 4 bowls and serve.

Helpful hint: The soup can be completed through step 1 up to 8 hours in advance. Return to a boil before proceeding.

Fat: 2g/7%
Calories: 267
Saturated Fat: 0.3g
Carbohydrate: 25g
Protein: 36g
Cholesterol: 73mg
Sodium: 693mg

Lemony soups made with rice (or rice-like orzo pasta) are typically Greek. The fresh lemon taste is perfect with fish.

CIOPPINO

SERVES: 4
WORKING TIME: 25 MINUTES
TOTAL TIME: 35 MINUTES

The varied ethnic populations of the city of San Francisco have contributed tremendously to the local cuisine. Cioppino was a creation of Italian-American fisherman and has been served in San Francisco restaurants since the turn of the century. Accompany this seafood stew with generous slabs of herbed garlic bread or warm Italian bread.

1 tablespoon olive oil
2 red bell peppers, cut into ½-inch squares
2 carrots, thinly sliced
4 cloves garlic, minced
1 cup dry red wine
2 large tomatoes, coarsely chopped
2 tablespoons no-salt-added tomato paste
1 cup bottled clam juice
½ teaspoon dried oregano
¼ teaspoon salt
¼ teaspoon red pepper flakes
16 littleneck clams or other small hard-shell clams, well scrubbed
½ pound large shrimp, shelled and deveined
½ pound flounder fillet, cut into 1-inch chunks

1. In a large skillet, heat the oil until hot but not smoking over medium heat. Add the bell peppers, carrots, and garlic and cook, stirring frequently, until the peppers are crisp-tender, about 4 minutes. Add the wine, bring to a boil, and cook until evaporated by half, about 4 minutes.

2. Stir in the tomatoes, tomato paste, clam juice, 1 cup of water, the oregano, salt, and red pepper flakes. Bring to a boil, add the clams, cover, and cook until the clams have opened, about 5 minutes. Remove the clams as they open and transfer them to 4 soup bowls; discard any that do not open.

3. Add the shrimp, cover, and cook for 2 minutes. Add the flounder, cover, and cook until the shrimp and flounder are just opaque, about 2 minutes. Transfer the shrimp and fish to the soup bowls, spoon in the broth and vegetables, and serve.

Helpful hint: On the East Coast, the smallest clams are properly called "little necks" (two words); clams of about the same size harvested in the West are called littlenecks (one word); Pacific littlenecks are also called rock clams. Any small hard-shell clam will work well in this recipe.

FAT: 6G/23%
CALORIES: 234
SATURATED FAT: 0.9G
CARBOHYDRATE: 15G
PROTEIN: 30G
CHOLESTEROL: 118MG
SODIUM: 441MG

Pungent green curries are a specialty of Thailand. This one is full of fresh, flavorful ingredients like scallions, cilantro, lime juice, ginger, and garlic. It's not as spicy as a traditional Thai curry, letting the wonderful delicacy of the crabmeat shine through. The white rice served alongside makes this delicious crab stew a meal in itself.

GREEN CURRY CRAB STEW

SERVES: 4
WORKING TIME: 30 MINUTES
TOTAL TIME: 40 MINUTES

1 cup long-grain rice

½ teaspoon salt

8 scallions, thickly sliced

¾ cup packed fresh cilantro or parsley sprigs

3 tablespoons fresh lime juice

4 cloves garlic, peeled

2 tablespoons coarsely chopped fresh ginger

1 tablespoon olive oil

1 pound all-purpose potatoes, peeled and cut into ¼-inch dice

1 red bell pepper, cut into ¼-inch squares

2 cups reduced-sodium chicken broth, defatted

¼ teaspoon freshly ground black pepper

⅛ teaspoon ground allspice

1 pound lump crabmeat, picked over to remove any cartilage (see tip)

1 cup frozen peas

1. In a medium saucepan, bring 2¼ cups of water to a boil. Add the rice and ¼ teaspoon of the salt, reduce to a simmer, cover, and cook until the rice is tender, about 17 minutes.

2. Meanwhile, in a food processor, combine the scallions, cilantro, lime juice, garlic, and ginger. Process to a smooth purée.

3. In a large skillet, heat the oil until hot but not smoking over medium heat. Add the potatoes and cook, stirring frequently, until lightly browned, about 5 minutes. Add the bell pepper and cook, stirring frequently, until crisp-tender, about 4 minutes. Add the scallion purée and cook until fragrant, about 1 minute.

4. Stir in the broth, black pepper, allspice, and the remaining ¼ teaspoon salt. Bring to a boil, reduce to a simmer, cover, and cook until the vegetables are tender, about 5 minutes. Gently stir in the crabmeat and peas, cover, and simmer until the crab and peas are warmed through, about 5 minutes. Divide the rice among 4 plates, spoon the stew alongside, and serve.

Helpful hint: This stew can be made with flounder fillets instead of the crabmeat. Use 1 pound of fish cut into 2-inch pieces. The cooking time remains the same.

FAT: 6G/12%
CALORIES: 439
SATURATED FAT: 0.8G
CARBOHYDRATE: 63G
PROTEIN: 32G
CHOLESTEROL: 114MG
SODIUM: 966MG

TIP

Lump crabmeat consists of large chunks of meat from the body (rather than the claws) of the crab. Before using lump crabmeat, whether fresh or canned, look it over carefully and remove any bits of cartilage or shell that may have remained in the meat. Don't over-handle the crabmeat or the "lumps" will fall apart.

SHRIMP AND CORN CHOWDER

SERVES: 4
WORKING TIME: 25 MINUTES
TOTAL TIME: 35 MINUTES

2 red bell peppers, halved lengthwise and seeded

2 teaspoons olive oil

2 ounces baked ham, diced

4 scallions, thinly sliced

¾ pound sweet potatoes, peeled and cut into ½-inch cubes

1½ cups reduced-sodium chicken broth, defatted

¾ teaspoon dried tarragon

½ teaspoon salt

¼ teaspoon freshly ground black pepper

⅛ teaspoon nutmeg

1 pound large shrimp, shelled, deveined, and halved crosswise

1½ cups frozen corn kernels

1 cup low-fat (1%) milk

2 teaspoons cornstarch mixed with 1 tablespoon water

1. Preheat the broiler. Place the bell pepper halves, cut-sides down, on the broiler rack. Broil the peppers 4 inches from the heat for 12 minutes, or until the skin is blackened. When the peppers are cool enough to handle, peel them and cut into ½-inch squares.

2. Meanwhile, in a Dutch oven or large saucepan, heat the oil until hot but not smoking over medium heat. Add the ham and scallions and cook, stirring occasionally, until the scallions are softened, about 2 minutes. Add the sweet potatoes, stirring until well coated. Add the broth, 1 cup of water, the tarragon, salt, black pepper, and nutmeg and bring to a boil. Reduce the heat to a simmer, cover, and cook until the sweet potatoes are tender, about 7 minutes.

3. Add the shrimp, corn, milk, and roasted bell peppers. Cover and simmer until the shrimp are just opaque, about 3 minutes. Bring to a boil, add the cornstarch mixture, and cook, stirring constantly, until slightly thickened, about 1 minute.

Helpful hint: You can roast and peel the peppers a day or two in advance and refrigerate them in a covered container until needed.

FAT: 6G/17%
CALORIES: 310
SATURATED FAT: 1.4G
CARBOHYDRATE: 37G
PROTEIN: 28G
CHOLESTEROL: 150MG
SODIUM: 866MG

Corn chowder is a Southern favorite, and so is fresh shrimp: This chowder combines the two. We've included sweet potatoes to reinforce the Southern theme, and you'll detect a delightful smoky flavor, too—it comes from roasted bell peppers and cubes of baked ham. Serve the confetti-colored chowder with thick slices of sourdough bread.

NEW ENGLAND FISH SOUP

SERVES: 4
WORKING TIME: 30 MINUTES
TOTAL TIME: 40 MINUTES

We've enlivened this homey soup with a jazzy French touch: A spoonful of garlicky mayonnaise (aïoli) stirred in before serving. When made from scratch, aïoli consists mainly of egg yolks and olive oil; we've saved time and cut quite a lot of fat by basing ours on prepared reduced-fat mayonnaise. Serve the soup with whole-grain crackers and a lettuce-and-tomato salad.

8 cloves garlic, peeled

2 tablespoons reduced-fat mayonnaise

2 tablespoons fresh lemon juice

1 tablespoon olive oil

6 tablespoons chopped Canadian bacon (2 ounces)

2 leeks, cut into ½-inch pieces

2 large carrots, halved lengthwise and thinly sliced

2 ribs celery, cut into ¼-inch-thick slices

½ pound red potatoes, cut into ¼-inch dice

½ cup bottled clam juice or reduced-sodium chicken broth, defatted

½ teaspoon salt

1 cup evaporated skimmed milk

1¼ pounds skinless cod fillets, cut into 2-inch chunks

¼ cup chopped fresh parsley

1. In a small pot of boiling water, cook the garlic for 3 minutes to blanch. Drain, transfer to a food processor or blender along with the mayonnaise and lemon juice, and process to a smooth purée.

2. In a Dutch oven or flameproof casserole, heat the oil until hot but not smoking over medium heat. Add the Canadian bacon and leeks and cook, stirring occasionally, until the leeks are softened, about 5 minutes. Add the carrots and celery and cook, stirring frequently, until the carrots are crisp-tender, about 4 minutes.

3. Add the potatoes, stirring to coat. Add the clam juice, 3 cups of water, and the salt and bring to a boil. Reduce to a simmer, cover, and cook until the potatoes are tender, about 5 minutes. Stir in the evaporated milk, bring to a boil, and add the cod. Reduce to a simmer and cook, uncovered, until the fish is just opaque, about 5 minutes. Add the garlic mixture, stirring until well combined. Ladle the soup into 4 bowls, sprinkle with the parsley, and serve.

Helpful hint: Cup for cup, evaporated skimmed milk contains a whopping 90 grams less fat than heavy cream.

FAT: 7G/18%
CALORIES: 350
SATURATED FAT: 1.3G
CARBOHYDRATE: 35G
PROTEIN: 36G
CHOLESTEROL: 71MG
SODIUM: 796MG

In Portugal, cooks often sauté slices of linguiça—a garlicky pork sausage—to get soups and stews off to a savory start. (We've substituted Spanish chorizo, which is very similar to linguiça but more widely available in the United States.) Golden cubes of butternut squash make a lovely change from potatoes in this stew.

PORTUGUESE FISH STEW

SERVES: 4
WORKING TIME: 25 MINUTES
TOTAL TIME: 40 MINUTES

3 ounces chorizo sausage (see tip), thinly sliced, or 3 ounces Canadian bacon, cut into julienne strips

1 onion, diced

3 cloves garlic, minced

1½ cups reduced-sodium chicken broth, defatted

½ cup dry white wine

2 cups peeled, cut butternut squash (1-inch cubes)

1 cup no-salt-added canned tomatoes, drained and chopped

1½ teaspoons paprika

1 teaspoon hot pepper sauce

¼ teaspoon salt

1 cup frozen corn kernels

1½ pounds sea bass, halibut, or flounder fillets, cut into 2-inch pieces

1. In a Dutch oven or flameproof casserole, combine the chorizo, onion, garlic, and ½ cup of the broth over medium heat. Cook, stirring frequently, until the onion is softened, about 7 minutes. Add the wine, increase the heat to high, and cook until almost evaporated, about 3 minutes.

2. Add the squash, stirring to coat. Add the remaining 1 cup broth, the tomatoes, paprika, hot pepper sauce, and salt. Reduce to a simmer, cover, and cook until the squash is tender, about 7 minutes. Stir in the corn, place the fish on top, cover, and cook until the fish is just opaque, about 4 minutes. Divide the stew among 4 bowls and serve.

Helpful hint: There is also a Mexican sausage called chorizo, but it differs from the Spanish type in that it is made from raw, rather than smoked, pork. If you can't find firm Spanish-style chorizo, use Canadian bacon instead.

TIP

Spanish-style chorizo is made from coarsely ground smoked pork, garlic, and spices. It is formed into links that are about ¾-inch in diameter and 8 inches long.

FAT: 12G/29%
CALORIES: 374
SATURATED FAT: 4G
CARBOHYDRATE: 26G
PROTEIN: 41G
CHOLESTEROL: 87MG
SODIUM: 695MG

CRAB BISQUE

SERVES: 4
WORKING TIME: 30 MINUTES
TOTAL TIME: 40 MINUTES

In our bisque, evaporated skimmed milk, bread crumbs, and tomato paste add the richness usually provided by loads of heavy cream.

2 teaspoons olive oil

1 onion, diced

3 cloves garlic, minced

2 carrots, thinly sliced

2 tablespoons Cognac or other brandy

½ cup dry white wine

Two 6-ounce cans crabmeat

2 cups reduced-sodium chicken broth, defatted

2 tablespoons no-salt-added tomato paste

½ teaspoon dried tarragon

⅛ teaspoon cayenne pepper

3 tablespoons plain dried bread crumbs

2 cups evaporated skimmed milk

2 tablespoons minced fresh chives or scallion greens

1. In a large nonstick saucepan, heat the oil until hot but not smoking over medium heat. Add the onion and garlic and cook, stirring frequently, until the onion is softened, about 7 minutes. Add the carrots and cook, stirring frequently, until they are tender, about 4 minutes.

2. Remove the pan from the heat, add the Cognac, and return the pan to the heat. Cook for 1 minute to evaporate the alcohol. Add the wine and cook, stirring, until almost evaporated, about 2 minutes.

3. Stir in the crabmeat, broth, tomato paste, tarragon, and cayenne and bring to a boil. Reduce the heat to a simmer, cover, and cook until the soup is richly flavored, about 5 minutes. Stir in the bread crumbs and evaporated milk and bring to a boil. Transfer the soup to a food processor and process to a smooth purée. Divide the soup among 4 bowls, sprinkle the chives over, and serve.

Helpful hint: Instead of transferring the vegetables to a food processor, you can use a hand blender right in the pot. Run the blender in on-and-off pulses until the soup is a smooth purée.

FAT: 4G/14%
CALORIES: 262
SATURATED FAT: 0.7G
CARBOHYDRATE: 30G
PROTEIN: 27G
CHOLESTEROL: 63MG
SODIUM: 752MG

BIG BATCHES

5

Irish Stew

SERVES: 8
WORKING TIME: 20 MINUTES
TOTAL TIME: 6 TO 8 HOURS

This hearty dinner for eight suggests all sorts of winter entertaining possibilities: A supper centering around this stew would be the perfect sequel to an afternoon of skating, skiing, or sledding. And the slow cooker does most of the work, so the meal is ready when you walk in the door. Serve it with Irish soda bread and some crisp, cold cider or ale.

2 tablespoons flour

1¼ teaspoons salt

¾ teaspoon dried thyme

¼ teaspoon freshly ground black pepper

1½ cups reduced-sodium chicken broth, defatted

2 pounds all-purpose potatoes, peeled and cut into 1-inch chunks

1½ pounds well-trimmed boneless lamb shoulder, cut into 1-inch chunks

¾ pound white turnips or rutabaga, peeled and cut into ½-inch chunks

4 leeks, halved lengthwise and cut into ½-inch-thick slices

3 carrots, halved lengthwise and cut into ½-inch-thick slices

6 cloves garlic, slivered

1½ cups frozen peas

½ cup chopped fresh parsley

1. In a large electric slow cooker, combine the flour, salt, thyme, and pepper. Stir in the broth until well combined. Add the potatoes, lamb, turnips, leeks, carrots, and garlic. Cover, and with the setting on low, cook, stirring once or twice, until the meat and vegetables are tender, 6 to 8 hours.

2. With the back of a spoon, mash some of the vegetables against the side of the pot to thicken the stew. Stir in the peas and parsley and cook, uncovered, until just heated through, about 2 minutes.

Helpful hint: Although rutabagas and turnips differ in size and color, the two vegetables are closely related—one can be substituted for the other in most recipes. Both are good sources of vitamin C.

FAT: 6G/19%
CALORIES: 282
SATURATED FAT: 2.1G
CARBOHYDRATE: 35G
PROTEIN: 22G
CHOLESTEROL: 56MG
SODIUM: 604MG

CHICKEN CURRY FOR A CROWD

SERVES: 8
WORKING TIME: 35 MINUTES
TOTAL TIME: 55 MINUTES

Instead of the expected pasta casserole, welcome friends with an exotic curry. For a relaxed party, do the prep work in advance—or make the curry ahead and reheat it while you cook the rice. This meal doesn't need much in the way of accompaniment, but you might offer mango chutney and perhaps a basket of warm mini-pitas, which resemble the Indian bread, "naan."

2 cups long-grain rice

1 teaspoon salt

¼ cup flour

¾ teaspoon freshly ground black pepper

2 pounds skinless, boneless chicken breasts, cut into 1-inch chunks

4 teaspoons olive oil

8 scallions, cut into 1-inch lengths

6 cloves garlic, minced

2 tablespoons minced fresh ginger

2 teaspoons curry powder

1½ teaspoons ground coriander

1 teaspoon ground cumin

¼ teaspoon ground cardamom

2 cups reduced-sodium chicken broth, defatted

1 pound red potatoes, cut into ½-inch cubes

2 cups peeled baby carrots

4 cups small cauliflower florets

3 tablespoons mango chutney

1. In a medium saucepan, bring 4½ cups of water to a boil. Add the rice and ¼ teaspoon of the salt, reduce to a simmer, cover, and cook until the rice is tender, about 17 minutes.

2. Meanwhile, on a sheet of waxed paper, combine the flour, ¼ teaspoon of the salt, and ¼ teaspoon of the pepper. Dredge the chicken in the flour mixture, shaking off the excess. In a large nonstick Dutch oven or flameproof casserole, heat 2 teaspoons of the oil until hot but not smoking over medium heat. Add half the chicken and cook until golden brown, about 2 minutes per side. With a slotted spoon, transfer the chicken to a plate. Repeat with the remaining 2 teaspoons oil and remaining chicken.

3. Add the scallions, garlic, and ginger to the pan and cook, stirring frequently, until the scallions are softened, about 2 minutes. Stir in the curry powder, coriander, cumin, cardamom, the remaining ½ teaspoon salt, and remaining ½ teaspoon pepper and cook until fragrant, about 1 minute.

4. Add the broth and 1 cup of water to the pan and bring to a boil. Add the potatoes and carrots, cover, and gently boil until the potatoes are almost tender, about 5 minutes. Stir in the cauliflower and chutney, cover, and cook until the vegetables are tender, about 5 minutes. Return the chicken to the pan and cook until just cooked through, about 3 minutes. Serve the curry with the rice.

FAT: 4G/8%
CALORIES: 433
SATURATED FAT: 0.8G
CARBOHYDRATE: 63G
PROTEIN: 34G
CHOLESTEROL: 66MG
SODIUM: 604MG

GREEN GAZPACHO WITH SPICED SHRIMP

SERVES: 8
WORKING TIME: 30 MINUTES
TOTAL TIME: 35 MINUTES PLUS CHILLING TIME

4 cloves garlic, minced

1 tablespoon paprika

¾ teaspoon salt

½ teaspoon freshly ground black pepper

1½ pounds large shrimp, shelled and deveined

4 ounces white sandwich bread (about 4 slices), torn into small pieces

1½ cups bottled clam juice

6 large cucumbers, unpeeled, thickly sliced

3 green bell peppers, cut into large chunks

2 red bell peppers, cut into large chunks

¾ cup cider vinegar

2¼ teaspoons dried tarragon

1. In a large bowl, combine the garlic, paprika, ¼ teaspoon of the salt, and ¼ teaspoon of the black pepper. Add the shrimp, tossing to coat well.

2. In a medium bowl, combine the bread and clam juice, tossing until the bread is well moistened. Transfer to a food processor along with the cucumbers, bell peppers, vinegar, tarragon, the remaining ½ teaspoon salt, and remaining ¼ teaspoon black pepper. Process to a coarse purée. Chill until ready to serve.

3. Just before serving, preheat the broiler or prepare the grill. Cook the shrimp 6 inches from the heat, turning once, for 4 minutes, or until just opaque. Halve the shrimp crosswise. Ladle the soup into 8 serving bowls, spoon the shrimp on top, and serve.

Helpful hints: Because cucumbers are often waxed, you may want to peel them before using them in this recipe, though the gazpacho will not be as brightly colored.

FAT: 2G/11%
CALORIES: 164
SATURATED FAT: 0.3G
CARBOHYDRATE: 20G
PROTEIN: 17G
CHOLESTEROL: 105MG
SODIUM: 496MG

Here's a cool way to serve an al fresco dinner: Make the soup (a no-tomato version of the Spanish classic) a day ahead of time and refrigerate it. When the guests arrive, fire up the barbecue and grill the shrimp. Ladle out the icy-cold soup, top it with the hot shrimp, and enjoy a relaxed outdoor meal. Bread sticks or French bread would go well with the gazpacho.

You'll love the mellow sweetness of braised onions and plump raisins in this cozy old-fashioned dish. Traditionally, a whole chicken is baked in the oven for an hour or two; but we've used boneless chicken breasts, turning this into an under-an-hour stovetop dish. Toss a simple salad to serve alongside for a complete meal.

138

SMOTHERED CHICKEN STEW

SERVES: 8
WORKING TIME: 25 MINUTES
TOTAL TIME: 45 MINUTES

⅓ cup flour

1 teaspoon salt

½ teaspoon freshly ground black pepper

8 skinless, boneless chicken breast halves (about 2 pounds total), cut crosswise into thirds

2 tablespoons olive oil

3 pounds Spanish onions (see tip), halved and thinly sliced

2 tablespoons sugar

2 teaspoons ground ginger

¾ teaspoon dried rosemary

2 cups reduced-sodium chicken broth, defatted

½ cup raisins

1. On a sheet of waxed paper, combine the flour, ¼ teaspoon of the salt, and ¼ teaspoon of the pepper. Dredge the chicken in the flour mixture, shaking off and reserving the excess.

2. In a large nonstick Dutch oven or flameproof casserole, heat 1 tablespoon of the oil until hot but not smoking. Add half the chicken and cook until golden brown, about 2 minutes per side. With a slotted spoon, transfer the chicken to a plate. Repeat with the remaining 1 tablespoon oil and remaining chicken.

3. Add the onions to the pan and sprinkle them with the sugar, ginger, and rosemary. Cook, stirring frequently, until the onions are lightly colored, about 5 minutes. Add 1 cup of water and cook, stirring frequently, until the onions are very tender, about 10 minutes.

4. Sprinkle the reserved flour mixture over the onions, stirring until well coated. Gradually add the broth, the remaining ¾ teaspoon salt, and remaining ¼ teaspoon pepper and bring to a boil. Reduce to a simmer, return the chicken to the pan, add the raisins, and cook, stirring occasionally, until the chicken is just cooked through, about 5 minutes. Divide the stew among 8 bowls and serve.

Helpful hint: This is a great make-ahead stew. It can be prepared up to 12 hours in advance, covered, refrigerated, and gently reheated when you're ready to serve it. Add a little chicken broth if it seems too dry.

FAT: 5G/16%
CALORIES: 288
SATURATED FAT: 0.8G
CARBOHYDRATE: 31G
PROTEIN: 31G
CHOLESTEROL: 66MG
SODIUM: 530MG

TIP

Spanish onions are quite a bit bigger than regular yellow globe onions. The skins of Spanish onions may be any color from yellow to purple, and their flavor is milder and sweeter than regular onions, making them ideal for this subtly flavored chicken stew. Bermuda onions or large red (Italian) onions can be substituted for Spanish onions.

LEMON CHICKEN STEW WITH GREEN OLIVES

SERVES: 8
WORKING TIME: 35 MINUTES
TOTAL TIME: 50 MINUTES

¼ cup flour

¾ teaspoon salt

½ teaspoon freshly ground black pepper

8 skinless bone-in chicken breast halves (about 2½ pounds total), halved crosswise

1 tablespoon olive oil

8 cloves garlic, minced

⅓ cup fresh lemon juice

2 cups reduced-sodium chicken broth, defatted

1¼ pounds all-purpose potatoes, peeled and cut into ½-inch cubes

19-ounce can chick-peas, rinsed and drained

8 small pimiento-stuffed green olives, thinly sliced

½ cup chopped fresh parsley

1. On a sheet of waxed paper, combine the flour, ¼ teaspoon of the salt, and ¼ teaspoon of the pepper. Dredge the chicken in the flour mixture, shaking off the excess.

2. In a large nonstick Dutch oven or flameproof casserole, heat 1½ teaspoons of the oil until hot but not smoking over medium heat. Add half the chicken and cook until golden brown, about 2 minutes per side. With a slotted spoon, transfer the chicken to a plate. Repeat with the remaining 1½ teaspoons oil and remaining chicken.

3. Add the garlic to the pan and cook, stirring, until fragrant, about 1 minute. Add the lemon juice, stirring to combine with the pan juices. Stir in the broth, ½ cup of water, the remaining ½ teaspoon salt, and remaining ¼ teaspoon pepper. Bring to a boil and add the potatoes. Reduce to a simmer and return the chicken to the pan, along with the chick-peas and olives. Cover and simmer until the chicken is cooked through, about 20 minutes. Sprinkle the parsley over and serve.

Helpful hint: As a change from parsley, sprinkle the finished stew with chopped chives or with another fresh herb, such as basil or mint.

FAT: 4G/15%
CALORIES: 235
SATURATED FAT: 0.6G
CARBOHYDRATE: 22G
PROTEIN: 26G
CHOLESTEROL: 54MG
SODIUM: 576MG

This is the perfect meal for a gray day—flavored with fresh lemon juice, green olives, and garlic, it brings its own brightness to the table. It's just what you'd expect of a dish with origins in the Mediterranean, where cerulean skies, strong sun, and bold flavors are the rule. Garnish the stew with lemon slices and serve it with a French baguette or ficelle.

Ham Soup with Beans and Greens

SERVES: 8
WORKING TIME: 30 MINUTES
TOTAL TIME: 50 MINUTES

The Southern way to cook greens requires a smoked ham hock, or some salt pork, which suffuses the greens with rich flavor, but also bathes them in fat. We've kept the smoky goodness in our healthier soup by using cubes of lean ham. Kidney beans, potatoes, and rutabaga soak up their share of the savory broth and make the soup a satisfying meal.

2 teaspoons olive oil

¾ pound reduced-sodium ham, cut into ½-inch dice

1 large onion, diced

3 leeks, halved and thinly sliced

8 cloves garlic, minced

1½ pounds all-purpose potatoes, peeled and cut into 1-inch cubes

1 pound rutabaga, peeled and cut into 1-inch chunks

16-ounce can red kidney beans, rinsed and drained

10-ounce package frozen chopped spinach, thawed

3 tablespoons red wine vinegar

1. In a nonstick Dutch oven or flameproof casserole, heat the oil until hot but not smoking over medium heat. Add the ham and cook, stirring frequently, until lightly browned, about 2 minutes. Add the onion, leeks, and garlic and cook, stirring frequently, until the vegetables are tender, about 7 minutes.

2. Add 6 cups of water and bring to a boil over medium heat. Add the potatoes and rutabaga, cover, and cook until the potatoes are firm-tender, about 10 minutes. Add the beans, spinach, and vinegar. Cover and cook until the spinach and beans are heated through, about 5 minutes.

Helpful hint: If you like, accent the Southern qualities of the soup by substituting the same amount of sweet potatoes for the white potatoes.

FAT: 3G/13%
CALORIES: 215
SATURATED FAT: 0.7G
CARBOHYDRATE: 34G
PROTEIN: 14G
CHOLESTEROL: 20MG
SODIUM: 472MG

LENTIL AND SAUSAGE SOUP

SERVES: 8
WORKING TIME: 30 MINUTES
TOTAL TIME: 1 HOUR

*L*entils, like split peas, take on a wonderful flavor when cooked with smoked meats. We've used Polish kielbasa for this hearty, tasty stew.

2 teaspoons olive oil

1 large onion, diced

4 cloves garlic, minced

3 carrots, halved lengthwise and thinly sliced

2 ribs celery, thinly sliced

1 pound lentils, rinsed and picked over

Three 14½-ounce cans no-salt-added stewed tomatoes, chopped with their juice

1 teaspoon salt

½ teaspoon freshly ground black pepper

¼ teaspoon ground allspice

10-ounce package frozen peas

½ pound kielbasa, thinly sliced

⅓ cup chopped fresh parsley

1. In a Dutch oven or flameproof casserole, heat the oil until hot but not smoking over medium heat. Add the onion and garlic and cook, stirring occasionally, until the onion is softened, about 7 minutes. Stir in the carrots and celery and cook, stirring occasionally, until the celery is softened, about 4 minutes.

2. Add the lentils, tomatoes, salt, pepper, allspice, and 4½ cups of water and bring to a boil over medium heat. Reduce to a simmer, cover, and cook until the lentils are tender, about 30 minutes. Stir in the peas, kielbasa, and parsley and cook just until heated through. Divide the soup among 8 bowls and serve.

Helpful hint: Kielbasa is a Polish smoked sausage sold in long, thick links. It's usually made from pork but sometimes contains beef as well; turkey kielbasa, a lower-fat alternative, is also available and can be substituted here.

FAT: 10G/23%
CALORIES: 389
SATURATED FAT: 3.1G
CARBOHYDRATE: 55G
PROTEIN: 24G
CHOLESTEROL: 19MG
SODIUM: 677MG

CREAM OF TOMATO-RICE SOUP

SERVES: 8
WORKING TIME: 20 MINUTES
TOTAL TIME: 35 MINUTES

¾ cup long-grain rice

1 teaspoon salt

1 tablespoon olive oil

6 scallions, chopped

¾ cup chopped fresh basil

6 cups drained, chopped no-salt-added canned tomatoes

2 cups reduced-sodium chicken broth, defatted

2 teaspoons sugar

¾ teaspoon ground ginger

¼ teaspoon nutmeg

2 cups evaporated low-fat milk

¾ teaspoon cornstarch

½ teaspoon baking soda

16-ounce can white kidney beans (cannellini), rinsed and drained

1. In a medium pot of boiling water, cook the rice with ¼ teaspoon of the salt for 10 minutes to partially cook. Drain well.

2. Meanwhile, in a Dutch oven, heat the oil until hot but not smoking over medium heat. Add the scallions and ½ cup of the basil and cook until the scallions are softened, about 2 minutes. Stir in the tomatoes, broth, sugar, ginger, nutmeg, and the remaining ¾ teaspoon salt. Bring to a boil, reduce to a simmer, cover, and cook until the soup is richly flavored, about 7 minutes. Ladle the soup into a large bowl. Working in batches, transfer the soup to a food processor and process to a smooth purée. Return the purée to the Dutch oven as you work.

3. In a small bowl, combine ½ cup of the evaporated milk and the cornstarch. Stir the baking soda, beans, and drained rice into the pan and bring to a boil over medium heat. Stir the cornstarch mixture into the Dutch oven, then gradually stir in the remaining 1½ cups evaporated milk. Cook, stirring, until the soup is slightly thickened and the beans and rice are just heated through, about 1 minute. Stir in the remaining ¼ cup basil, divide the soup among 8 bowls, and serve.

Helpful hint: Both the sugar and the baking soda help counteract the natural acidity of the tomatoes to produce a smooth, rounded flavor with no trace of sourness.

FAT: 4G/17%
CALORIES: 218
SATURATED FAT: 0.4G
CARBOHYDRATE: 36G
PROTEIN: 11G
CHOLESTEROL: 10MG
SODIUM: 698MG

Not just rice, but also creamy white beans balance the tangy tomato taste of this basil-scented soup.

BARBECUED BEEF STEW

SERVES: 8
WORKING TIME: 30 MINUTES
TOTAL TIME: 45 MINUTES

The down-home flavor of barbecue is most welcome in a hunger-chasing stew. Spicy but not hot (unless you care to toss in some extra cayenne), this dish has vegetables built right in; and instead of the usual chopped or shredded meat, this stew is filled with good-sized cubes of beef. Bake up some cornsticks, corn muffins, or corn bread to serve alongside.

¼ cup flour

¾ teaspoon salt

2 pounds well-trimmed top round of beef, cut into ½-inch cubes

4 teaspoons olive oil

5 cloves garlic, minced

14½-ounce can no-salt-added stewed tomatoes, chopped with their juice

Two 8-ounce cans no-salt-added tomato sauce

2 tablespoons molasses

1 teaspoon ground ginger

1 teaspoon dried oregano

1 teaspoon Worcestershire sauce

¼ teaspoon cayenne pepper

1¼ pounds green beans, cut into 1-inch lengths

10-ounce package frozen corn kernels

1. On a sheet of waxed paper, combine the flour and ¼ teaspoon of the salt. Dredge the beef in the flour mixture, shaking off the excess.

2. In a large nonstick Dutch oven or flameproof casserole, heat 2 teaspoons of the oil until hot but not smoking over medium heat. Add half the beef and cook until lightly browned, about 4 minutes. With a slotted spoon, transfer the beef to a plate. Repeat with the remaining 2 teaspoons oil and remaining beef.

3. Add the garlic and cook, stirring frequently, until fragrant, about 2 minutes. Stir in the stewed tomatoes, tomato sauce, molasses, ginger, oregano, Worcestershire, cayenne, and the remaining ½ teaspoon salt and bring to a boil. Reduce to a simmer, cover, and cook for 5 minutes to blend the flavors.

4. Stir in the green beans and simmer, uncovered, until the beans are tender, about 6 minutes. Return the beef to the pan, add the corn, and simmer just until the beef is cooked through and the corn is hot, about 3 minutes. Divide the stew among 8 bowls and serve.

Helpful hint: You can use a 10-ounce package of frozen green beans instead of the fresh green beans if you like; add the frozen beans along with the corn, and allow an extra minute or two for the vegetables to heat through.

FAT: 7G/22%
CALORIES: 283
SATURATED FAT: 1.7G
CARBOHYDRATE: 28G
PROTEIN: 30G
CHOLESTEROL: 65MG
SODIUM: 301MG

An
intense triple-
mushroom flavor
makes this light but
rich-tasting soup
unique. Based on a
dried-mushroom broth
enhanced with sherry,
the soup brims with
slices of the familiar
button mushrooms as
well as meaty-tasting
fresh shiitakes. Serve it,
with lightly toasted
slices of French bread,
as the first course of a
roast turkey or chicken
dinner.

THREE-MUSHROOM SOUP

SERVES: 8
WORKING TIME: 35 MINUTES
TOTAL TIME: 55 MINUTES

½ ounce dried mushrooms
(see tip)

1½ cups boiling water

2 teaspoons olive oil

2 onions, diced

6 cloves garlic, minced

3 carrots, halved lengthwise and
thinly sliced

2½ pounds fresh button
mushrooms, thinly sliced

1 pound fresh shiitake
mushrooms, thinly sliced

⅓ cup dry sherry

3½ cups reduced-sodium beef
broth

½ teaspoon ground ginger

½ teaspoon salt

½ teaspoon freshly ground black
pepper

2 cups low-fat (1%) milk

2 tablespoons cornstarch mixed
with 3 tablespoons water

½ cup snipped fresh dill

1. In a small bowl, combine the dried mushrooms and the boiling water and let stand until softened, about 10 minutes. Scoop the dried mushrooms from their soaking liquid, reserve the liquid, then rinse and coarsely chop the mushrooms. Strain the liquid through a paper towel-lined sieve.

2. In a large nonstick saucepan or Dutch oven, heat the oil until hot but not smoking over medium heat. Add the onions and garlic and cook, stirring frequently, until the onions are golden, about 4 minutes. Add ½ cup of the mushroom soaking liquid and cook until the onions are softened, about 4 minutes. Add the carrots, stirring to coat. Add the remaining mushroom soaking liquid and cook, stirring frequently, until the carrots are tender, about 4 minutes.

3. Stir in the chopped soaked mushrooms and the fresh button and shiitake mushrooms. Cover and cook, stirring frequently, until the mushrooms are softened, about 5 minutes. Add the sherry, increase the heat to high, and cook until the sherry has evaporated, about 3 minutes. Stir in the broth, 1 cup of water, the ginger, salt, and pepper. Bring to a boil, reduce to a simmer, cover, and cook until the soup is richly flavored, about 7 minutes.

4. Stir in the milk and bring to a boil. Add the cornstarch mixture and cook, stirring constantly, until slightly thickened, about 1 minute. Stir in the dill, ladle into 8 bowls, and serve.

FAT: 3G/17%
CALORIES: 163
SATURATED FAT: 0.7G
CARBOHYDRATE: 26G
PROTEIN: 9G
CHOLESTEROL: 2MG
SODIUM: 465MG

TIP

"Generic" dried mushrooms like these, imported from various countries, are sold in most supermarkets. Their low price belies their powerfully concentrated flavor. Gourmet shops offer fancier dried mushrooms, including porcini, shiitakes, and morels, at considerably higher prices.

HEARTY TURKEY CHOWDER

SERVES: 8
WORKING TIME: 35 MINUTES
TOTAL TIME: 45 MINUTES

1 tablespoon olive oil

6 tablespoons chopped Canadian bacon (2 ounces)

1 large onion, diced

2 leeks, halved lengthwise and thinly sliced

2 green bell peppers, cut into ½-inch squares

3 cups reduced-sodium chicken broth, defatted

½ teaspoon dried rosemary

½ teaspoon dried thyme

½ teaspoon freshly ground black pepper

½ teaspoon salt

1½ pounds all-purpose potatoes, peeled and cut into ½-inch cubes

2 pounds skinless, boneless turkey breast, cut into ½-inch chunks

1 cup frozen peas

¾ cup canned sliced water chestnuts, drained (optional)

1½ cups evaporated skimmed milk

2 tablespoons cornstarch mixed with 3 tablespoons water

1. In a large Dutch oven or flameproof casserole, heat the oil until hot but not smoking over medium heat. Add the Canadian bacon, onion, and leeks and cook, stirring frequently, until the onion is softened, about 7 minutes.

2. Add the bell peppers and cook, stirring frequently, until softened, about 5 minutes. Stir in the broth, 3 cups of water, the rosemary, thyme, black pepper, and salt and bring to a boil. Add the potatoes and turkey, reduce the heat to a simmer, and cook until the soup is richly flavored and the vegetables are tender, about 7 minutes.

3. Stir in the peas, water chestnuts, and evaporated milk and return to a boil. Add the cornstarch mixture and cook, stirring constantly, until the soup is creamy, about 1 minute.

Helpful hint: If making the chowder in advance, complete steps 1 and 2; cool, cover, and refrigerate. At serving time, reheat the chowder to a simmer and then continue with step 3.

FAT: 3G/9%
CALORIES: 310
SATURATED FAT: 0.7G
CARBOHYDRATE: 32G
PROTEIN: 38G
CHOLESTEROL: 76MG
SODIUM: 622MG

The holiday season brings many opportunities for entertaining: An informal gathering of close friends would offer a welcome respite from the seasonal bustle, and a steaming pot of turkey chowder is the perfect dish for the occasion. Along with turkey and leeks, this chowder has a smoky undertone of Canadian bacon and the surprising crunch of water chestnuts.

SUPER BOWL CHILI

SERVES: 8
WORKING TIME: 25 MINUTES
TOTAL TIME: 6 TO 8 HOURS

You don't have to be a football fan to love this slow-cooked pork-and-beef chili, but many passionate partisans of the game have come to see a bowl of chili as a natural part of the proceedings. You can bet, though, that just about any hungry group would welcome the chili with equal enthusiasm. This is a mild chili; if you like yours hot, add extra chili powder, or serve hot sauce on the side.

¾ cup dried kidney beans, rinsed and picked over

¾ cup dried black beans, rinsed and picked over

1 pound well-trimmed pork tenderloin, cut into ½-inch chunks

1 pound well-trimmed top round of beef, cut into ½-inch chunks

Two 14½-ounce cans no-salt-added stewed tomatoes, chopped with their juice

Two 8-ounce cans no-salt-added tomato sauce

1 large onion, diced

1 red bell pepper, cut into ½-inch squares

1 green bell pepper, cut into ½-inch squares

6 cloves garlic, slivered

1 tablespoon chili powder

1½ teaspoons ground cumin

1½ teaspoons dried oregano

1½ teaspoons salt

1. In a medium pot, combine the dried beans with enough water to cover them by 2 inches. Bring to a boil, boil for 2 minutes, cover, and let stand for 1 hour. Drain well.

2. In a large electric slow cooker, combine the drained beans, pork, beef, stewed tomatoes, tomato sauce, 2 cups of water, the onion, bell peppers, garlic, chili powder, cumin, oregano, and salt. Stir together until well combined. Cover, and with the setting on low, cook until the beans and meats are tender and the chili is richly flavored, 6 to 8 hours. Divide the chili among 8 bowls and serve.

Helpful hint: To save time in the morning, soak the beans overnight: Place them in a bowl with water to cover by 2 inches, cover, and refrigerate. The next morning, drain the beans and assemble the stew in the slow cooker.

FAT: 5G/14%
CALORIES: 331
SATURATED FAT: 1.4G
CARBOHYDRATE: 38G
PROTEIN: 35G
CHOLESTEROL: 69MG
SODIUM: 517MG

GLOSSARY

Allspice—A dark, round, dried berry about the size of a peppercorn, called allspice because it tastes like a blend of cloves, cinnamon, and nutmeg. Usually sold in ground form, allspice is often mistakenly thought to be a mix of several spices.

Barley, quick-cooking—A form of barley that is thoroughly milled to remove the husk and bran layer, and then pre-steamed, so that it cooks in about 12 minutes rather than the 55 minutes required for pearl barley. Quick-cooking barley is no less nutritious than pearl barley, and is an excellent ingredient for hearty, low-fat soups.

Basil—An herb with a flavor between clove and licorice. Fresh basil will retain more fragrance if added at the end of cooking; dried basil can be used to advantage in soups, stews, and sauces. Store fresh basil by placing the stems in a container of water and covering the leaves loosely with a plastic bag.

Bay leaf—The dried, whole leaf of the evergreen European laurel tree. The herb adds a distinctive, pungent flavor to soups, stews, and casseroles; the Turkish variety is milder than the somewhat harsh California bay leaves. Always remove bay leaves before serving food.

Bean sprouts—The small shoots of mung, soy, or other beans. Widely used in Asian cooking, fresh bean sprouts are sold in Asian markets and in the produce sections of many supermarkets; canned bean sprouts are widely available, but they lack the crispness and clean flavor of fresh sprouts. Bean sprouts should be minimally cooked so that they retain their delicate, crisp texture.

Beans, canned—The rehydrated, ready-to-use form of dried beans. Many types of beans—black beans, red kidney beans,

cannellini, garbanzos, pinto beans—are available in this form, and they are great time-savers for soup-making. Always rinse and drain canned beans before using to remove the high-sodium canning liquid and freshen the beans' flavor.

Beans, dried—The seeds of a variety of pod-bearing plants, in dehydrated form. Dried beans require soaking and fairly long cooking, but they turn out firmer and fresher-tasting than canned beans. Dried beans are good candidates for soups made in a slow cooker. To presoak dried beans overnight, place them in a pot with cold water to cover by 2 inches, then set aside to soak for at least six hours (refrigerate them in warm weather). For quick soaking, bring the water to a boil and cook for 2 minutes, then let the beans soak for 1 hour. Either way, discard the soaking water before using the beans.

Canadian bacon—A lean smoked meat, similar to ham. This bacon is precooked, so it can be used as is. (For extra flavor, cook it in a skillet until the edges are lightly crisped.) Just a small amount adds big flavor to soups and stews, but with much less fat than regular bacon.

Cardamom—An aromatic spice that belongs to the ginger family. One of the components of curry powder, cardamom is frequently used in baking as well, especially in Scandinavian recipes. It is available ground or as whole seeds or pods.

Cayenne pepper—A hot spice ground from dried red chili peppers. Add cayenne to taste when preparing Mexican, Tex-Mex, Indian, Chinese, and Caribbean dishes; start with just a small amount, as cayenne is fiery-hot.

Chili powder—A commercially prepared seasoning mixture made from ground dried chilies, oregano, cumin, coriander, salt, and dehydrated garlic, and sometimes cloves and allspice; used in chilis and stews

for a Southwestern punch. Chili powders can range in strength from mild to very hot; their flavor fades over time, so buy a fresh jar if yours is more than 1 year old.

Cinnamon—The dried bark of a tropical tree, sold in rolled sticks or in ground form. This spice imparts a sweet, warm flavor that provides an intriguing counterpoint to savory seasonings in Middle Eastern and North African cooking.

Clam juice, bottled—A convenient form of clam juice. It adds a briny flavor to seafood sauces, soups, and chowders. If using canned clams or oysters rather than fresh, the addition of bottled clam juice intensifies the seafood flavor. If clam juice is unavailable, you can substitute chicken broth.

Cumin—A pungent, peppery-tasting spice essential to many Middle Eastern, Asian, Mexican, and Mediterranean dishes. Available ground or as whole seeds; the spice can be toasted in a dry skillet to bring out its flavor.

Curry powder—Not one spice but a mix of spices, commonly used in Indian cooking to flavor a dish with sweet heat and add a characteristic yellow-orange color. While curry blends vary (consisting of as many as 20 herbs and spices), they typically include turmeric (for its vivid yellow color), fenugreek, ginger, cardamom, cloves, cumin, coriander, and cayenne pepper. Commercially available Madras curry is hotter than other store-bought types.

Evaporated milk, skimmed and low-fat—Canned, unsweetened, homogenized milk that has had most of its fat removed: In the skimmed version, 100 percent of the fat has been removed; the low-fat version contains 1 percent fat. Used in soups, these products add a creamy richness with almost no fat. Store at room temperature for up to 6 months until opened, then refrigerate for up to 1 week.

Fennel—A vegetable resembling a flattened head of celery, with a subtle licorice flavor. The feathery fronds that top the stalks are used as an herb, and the bulb is used both raw and cooked, like celery. Choose firm, unblemished fennel bulbs with fresh green fronds. Store in the refrigerator in a plastic bag for three to four days. Fennel seeds, which come from a slightly different plant, have an almost sweet, licorice-like taste; they are often used in Italian dishes and with fish.

Garlic—The edible bulb of a plant closely related to onions, leeks, and chives. Garlic can be pungently assertive or sweetly mild, depending on how it is prepared: Minced or crushed garlic yields a more powerful flavor than whole or halved cloves. Whereas sautéing turns garlic rich and savory, slow simmering or roasting produces a mild, mellow flavor. Select firm, plump heads with dry skins; avoid heads that have begun to sprout. Store garlic in an open or loosely covered container in a cool, dark place for up to 2 months.

Ginger, fresh—A thin-skinned root used as a seasoning. Fresh ginger adds sweet pungency to Asian and Indian dishes. Tightly wrapped, unpeeled fresh ginger can be refrigerated for 1 week or frozen for up to 6 months. Ground ginger is not a true substitute for fresh, but it will lend a warming flavor to soups and stews.

Leek—A mild-flavored member of the onion family that resembles a giant scallion. Buy leeks with firm bottoms and fresh-looking tops; store them, loosely wrapped in plastic, in the refrigerator. To prepare, trim the root end and any blemished dark green leaves. Split the leek lengthwise, then rinse thoroughly to remove any dirt trapped between the leaves.

Lentil—A tiny, flat pulse (the dried seed of a legume), distinguished by a mild, nutty flavor and a starchy texture. The advantage of using lentils is that, unlike dried beans, they require no presoaking. They do require careful cooking, however, since overcooking makes them mushy. Beside the familiar brown variety, also try colorful green and red lentils in soups and stews.

Marjoram—A member of the mint family that tastes like mildly sweet oregano. Fresh marjoram should be added at the end of cooking so the flavor doesn't vanish. Dried marjoram, sold in leaf and ground form (the more intense leaf being preferable), stands up to longer cooking.

Mint—A large family of herbs used to impart a refreshingly heady fragrance and cool aftertaste to foods; the most common types are spearmint and peppermint. As with other fresh herbs, mint is best added toward the end of the cooking time. Dried mint is fairly intense, so a small amount goes a long way. Store fresh mint the same way as fresh basil.

Nutmeg—The hard, brown, nutlike seed of the nutmeg tree. Although mainly used in sweet dishes, nutmeg also complements green vegetables such as broccoli and spinach. Ground nutmeg is convenient, but the flavor of freshly grated nutmeg is far superior. This whole spice keeps almost indefinitely, and you grate can it freshly as needed on a special nutmeg grater or an ordinary box grater.

Okra—A finger-sized, tapered green pod vegetable with a flavor reminiscent of asparagus. When cooked in liquid, okra acts as a thickener, adding body with no extra fat. It's a favorite in Southern cooking, especially for gumbos. If using fresh, choose plump, firm, bright green pods no more than 3 inches long and store in the refrigerator, unwashed, for up to 2 days.

Paprika—A spice ground from a variety of red peppers and used in many traditional Hungarian and Spanish dishes. Paprika colors foods a characteristic brick-red and flavors dishes from sweet to spicy-hot, depending on the pepper potency. Like all pepper-based spices, paprika loses its color and flavor with time; check your supply and replace it if necessary.

Parsnip—A carrot-shaped beige root vegetable with a nut-like, slightly sweet flavor. Refrigerate parsnips, unwashed, in a perforated plastic bag for up to 1 week, or longer if they remain firm. Peel them before using.

Potatoes—Starchy, mild-flavored root vegetables with white flesh and tan to deep-red skin. Potatoes are classified by their intended use. Baking potatoes, such as russets, have thick skins and are best for baking, but being the starchiest of all potatoes, they are also good for thickening soups and stews. All-purpose potatoes, including long whites and round whites, are of medium starchiness and can be cooked in many ways, as their name indicates. Boiling potatoes are waxy and hold their shape when sliced into stews (or used in salads). Diminutive round red potatoes, sold when they are freshly dug and have not been stored, are called "new potatoes." It's best to store potatoes in a cool, dark place (not in the refrigerator).

Red pepper flakes—A spice made from a variety of dried red chili peppers. Pepper flakes will permeate a stew or a casserole with a burst of heat and flavor during the cooking and eating. Begin with a small amount—you can always add more.

Rosemary—An aromatic herb with needle-like leaves and a sharp pine-citrus flavor. Rosemary's robust flavor complements lamb particularly well, and it stands up to long cooking better than most herbs. If you can't get fresh rosemary, use whole dried leaves, which retain the flavor of the fresh herb quite well. Crush or chop rosemary leaves with a mortar and pestle or a chef's knife.

Rutabaga—A larger, rounder relative of the turnip, with a thick skin and deep-yellow flesh. Rutabagas can be used interchangeably with turnips, but their flesh is rich in beta carotene (turnips have none), so there is an advantage to seeking them out. The purplish-tan skin of rutabagas is almost always heavily waxed, so this vegetable should be pared with a sharp knife before using. Rutabagas will keep in the refrigerator for two weeks or more.

Sage—An intensely fragrant herb with grayish-green leaves. Sage will infuse a dish with a pleasant, musty mint taste; it's especially good with poultry. In its dried form, sage is sold as whole leaves, ground, and in a fluffy "rubbed" version. For the best flavor from the dried herb, buy whole leaves and crush them yourself.

Sherry—A fortified wine originally made in Spain. With its delicate nutlike flavor, sherry is a versatile cooking ingredient. When added to soups, especially toward the end of the cooking, it adds a lovely winy fragrance. Sherries range from dry to sweet; dry sherries are best for cooking.

Spanish onions—Large, spherical mild-flavored onions with skins that may be gold, red, or purple. Spanish onions have less of a harsh bite than regular globe onions, so they may be used raw (in salads or sandwiches) as well as for cooking. Bermuda onions or large red (Italian) onions can be substituted for Spanish onions.

Squash, butternut—A large, lightbulb-shaped winter squash. This firm-fleshed, starchy vegetable can be baked, boiled, or steamed; it adds substance and bright orange color to soups and stews. Pick an unbruised squash with no dark or soft spots and store it in a cool place for up to a month. Use a large, heavy knife to cut the squash; it can be peeled either before or after cooking.

Sweet potato—A tuber with sweet yellow or orange flesh, sometimes mistakenly called a yam. When added to soups, stews, or casseroles, sweet potatoes impart rich body and a distinctive orange color. They also contribute vitamin C and a good deal of beta carotene. Choose smooth-skinned potatoes with tapered ends and no blemishes. Store sweet potatoes in a cool, dark place (not in the refrigerator) for up to 1 month; they'll stay fresh for a week at room temperature.

Tarragon—A potent, sweet herb with a licorice- or anise-like taste. Dried tarragon loses its flavor quickly; check its potency by crushing a little between your fingers and sniffing for the strong aroma. As with most herbs, you may substitute 1 teaspoon dried for each tablespoon of fresh.

Thyme—A lemony-tasting member of the mint family frequently paired with bay leaves in Mediterranean-style and rice-based dishes. The dried herb, both ground and leaf, is an excellent substitute for the fresh.

Tofu—A soft, creamy white soybean product that is high in protein. A staple of most Asian cuisines, tofu (also called bean curd) can be sliced or cubed for use in soups; since its flavor is neutral, it works with many ingredients and seasonings. For the recipes in this book, use firm tofu, which looks like little pillows, rather than soft tofu, which comes in straight-edged blocks; soft tofu would crumble apart if cooked in liquid. For freshness, purchase packaged, vacuum-sealed tofu. Once opened, immerse in fresh, cold water, cover tightly, and refrigerate: Use within 5 days, changing the water daily.

Tomato paste—A concentrated essence of cooked tomatoes, sold in cans and tubes. Tomato paste is commonly used to thicken and accent the flavor and color of sauces; however, it is slightly bitter and should not be used alone or in large quantities. Cooking tomato paste mellows it. If you're using only part of a can of tomato paste, save the remainder by freezing it in a plastic bag.

Turnip—A winter root vegetable commonly used in soups and stews for its bitter sweet flavor and slight crunch. Available all year round, turnips have a peak season from October to February. When shopping, look for small turnips with unblemished skins; they have the mildest flavor.

Zucchini—A delicately flavored summer squash that looks like a cucumber with a speckled skin. The golden version of this squash makes a nice change: Its flesh is more yellow than that of regular zucchini, but the flavor is about the same.

INDEX

TIME-LIFE BOOKS

Time-Life Books is a division of Time Life Inc.

PRESIDENT and CEO: John M. Fahey Jr.

TIME-LIFE BOOKS

MANAGING EDITOR: Roberta Conlan

Director of Design: Michael Hentges
Editorial Production Manager: Ellen Robling
Senior Editors: Russell B. Adams Jr., Janet Cave, Lee Hassig,
    Robert Somerville, Henry Woodhead
Special Projects Editor: Rita Thievon Mullin
Director of Operations: Eileen Bradley
Director of Photography and Research: John Conrad Weiser
Library: Louise D. Forstall

PRESIDENT: John D. Hall

Vice President, Director of New Product Development: Neil Kagan
Associate Director, New Product Development: Quentin S. McAndrew
Marketing Director, New Product Development: Robin B. Shuster
Vice President, Book Production: Marjann Caldwell
Production Manager: Marlene Zack
Consulting Editor: Catherine Boland Hackett

Design for Great Taste~Low Fat by David Fridberg of
Miles Fridberg Molinaroli, Inc.

 REBUS, INC.
PUBLISHER: Rodney M. Friedman
EDITORIAL DIRECTOR: Charles L. Mee

Editorial Staff for *Hearty Soups & Stews*
Director, Recipe Development and Photography: Grace Young
Editorial Director: Kate Slate
Senior Recipe Developer: Sandra Rose Gluck
Recipe Developer: Paul Piccuito
Writer: Bonnie J. Slotnick
Managing Editor: Julee Binder Shapiro
Associate Editor: Rebecca Porter
Editorial Assistant: James W. Brown, Jr.
Nutritionists: Hill Nutrition Associates

Art Director: Timothy Jeffs
Photographer: Lisa Koenig
Photographers' Assistants: Rainer Fehringer, Petra Liebetanz
Food Stylists: A.J. Battifarano, Karen Pickus, Karen Tack
Assistant Food Stylists: Charles Davis, Susan Kadel, Amy Lord,
    Ellie Ritt
Prop Stylist: Debrah Donahue
Prop Coordinator: Karin Martin

Special thanks to Chantal Cookware Corporation

Library of Congress Cataloging-in-Publication Data

Hearty soups & stews.
    p.   cm.   -- (Great taste, low fat)
Includes index.
ISBN 0-7835-4559-2
1. Soups. 2. Stews. 3. Low-fat diet--Recipes. 4. Quick and easy
cookery. I. Time-Life Books. II. Series.
TX757.H39   1996
641.8'13--dc20
                                                            96-10640
                                                            CIP

Other Publications
THE TIME-LIFE COMPLETE GARDENER
HOME REPAIR AND IMPROVEMENT
JOURNEY THROUGH THE MIND AND BODY
WEIGHT WATCHERS® SMART CHOICE RECIPE COLLECTION
TRUE CRIME
THE AMERICAN INDIANS
THE ART OF WOODWORKING
LOST CIVILIZATIONS
ECHOES OF GLORY
THE NEW FACE OF WAR
HOW THINGS WORK
WINGS OF WAR
CREATIVE EVERYDAY COOKING
COLLECTOR'S LIBRARY OF THE UNKNOWN
CLASSICS OF WORLD WAR II
TIME-LIFE LIBRARY OF CURIOUS AND UNUSUAL FACTS
VOYAGE THROUGH THE UNIVERSE
THE THIRD REICH
MYSTERIES OF THE UNKNOWN
TIME FRAME
FIX IT YOURSELF
FITNESS, HEALTH & NUTRITION
SUCCESSFUL PARENTING
HEALTHY HOME COOKING
UNDERSTANDING COMPUTERS
LIBRARY OF NATIONS
THE ENCHANTED WORLD
THE KODAK LIBRARY OF CREATIVE PHOTOGRAPHY
GREAT MEALS IN MINUTES
THE CIVIL WAR
PLANET EARTH
THE EPIC OF FLIGHT
THE GOOD COOK
WORLD WAR II
THE OLD WEST

*For information on and a full description of any of the Time-Life Books series
listed above, please call 1-800-621-7026 or write:*
Reader Information
Time-Life Customer Service
P.O. Box C-32068
Richmond, Virginia 23261-2068

METRIC CONVERSION CHARTS

VOLUME EQUIVALENTS
(fluid ounces/milliliters and liters)

US	Metric
1 tsp	5 ml
1 tbsp (½ fl oz)	15 ml
¼ cup (2 fl oz)	60 ml
⅓ cup	80 ml
½ cup (4 fl oz)	120 ml
⅔ cup	160 ml
¾ cup (6 fl oz)	180 ml
1 cup (8 fl oz)	240 ml
1 qt (32 fl oz)	950 ml
1 qt + 3 tbsps	1 L
1 gal (128 fl oz)	4 L

Conversion formula
Fluid ounces x 30 = milliliters
1000 milliliters = 1 liter

WEIGHT EQUIVALENTS
(ounces and pounds/grams and kilograms)

US	Metric
¼ oz	7 g
½ oz	15 g
¾ oz	20 g
1 oz	30 g
8 oz (½ lb)	225 g
12 oz (¾ lb)	340 g
16 oz (1 lb)	455 g
35 oz (2.2 lbs)	1 kg

Conversion formula
Ounces x 28.35 = grams
1000 grams = 1 kilogram

LINEAR EQUIVALENTS
(inches and feet/centimeters and meters)

US	Metric
¼ in	.75 cm
½ in	1.5 cm
¾ in	2 cm
1 in	2.5 cm
6 in	15 cm
12 in (1 ft)	30 cm
39 in	1 m

Conversion formula
Inches x 2.54 = centimeters
100 centimeters = 1 meter

TEMPERATURE EQUIVALENTS
(Fahrenheit/Celsius)

US	Metric
0° (freezer temperature)	-18°
32° (water freezes)	0°
98.6°	37°
180° (water simmers*)	82°
212° (water boils*)	100°
250° (low oven)	120°
350° (moderate oven)	175°
425° (hot oven)	220°
500° (very hot oven)	260°

*at sea level

Conversion formula
Degrees Fahrenheit minus
32 ÷ 1.8 = degrees Celsius